SUGAR-FREE GLUTEN-FREE BAKING and DESSERTS

SUGAR-FREE GLUTEN-FREE BAKING and DESSERTS

Recipes for Healthy and Delicious Cookies, Cakes, Muffins, Scones, Pies, Puddings, Breads, and Pizzas

Kelly E. Keough

Ulysses Press

Published by Ulysses Press
          P.O. Box 3440
          Berkeley, CA 94703
          www.ulyssespress.com

An earlier version of this book, entitled *The Sweet Truth: A Sugar-free/Wheat-free Kitchen*, was published by BookSurge Publishing

ISBN: 978-1-56975-704-8
Library of Congress Catalog Number 2008911763

Printed in Canada by Webcom

 9 8 7 6 5 4 3 2

Acquisitions Editor: Nick Denton-Brown
Managing Editor: Claire Chun
Editors: Jennifer Privateer, Lauren Harrison
Indexer: Sayre Van Young
Cover design: DiAnna Van Eycke
Cover photo: © istockphoto.com/Paul Velgos
Interior design: what!design @ whatweb.com
Production: Judith Metzener, Abby Reser

Distributed by Publishers Group West

This self-help cookbook is dedicated to everyone who has ever healed the Self and continues to do so.

TABLE OF CONTENTS

ACKNOWLEDGMENTS

This self-help cookbook is dedicated to everyone who has ever healed the Self and continues to do so, for this book is a blueprint for personal healing from sugar addiction and compulsive overeating using food as an inspirational tool. The healing for me is an ongoing process and journey of discovery that has no destination, diet plan, or number on a scale, just a clear path of ascension rooted in optimal health and a pleasurable and joyful relationship with the sweets that I eat.

This cookbook is dedicated to my mother. She taught me how to cook. And also to my great-grandmother, Louise Schwert, a private cook for the rich who lived on Lake Erie. Gran handwrote all her own recipes in a notebook and that notebook became her cookbook that has been passed down from generation to generation. I took three of Gran's recipes (Cry Babies, Gran's Strawberry Rhubarb Pie, and Mocha Maca Crumb Cake) and transposed them Sweet Truth style into sugar-free, gluten-free desserts. I wish Gran would have known then what I know now about sugar-free alternatives, because she died of diabetes without even knowing she had the disease. Diabetes runs in my family. Because of this, every day I make a consistent decision to satisfy my sweet tooth with low-glycemic dishes and desserts and to do the exercise that I love: ballet, salsa, yoga, and surfing.

This book is especially dedicated to my grandmother (better known as Nana), Eleanor Chiavetta, of Chiavetta's Catering in Brant, NY. From the time I was born she always told me I could be anything I want to be—and let me tell you, being a sugar-free chef was the furthest thing from my mind. In fact, there really was no such thing as a sugar-free chef when she would sing that hopeful mantra to me as I went off to summer day camp with my sacred grape soda. Sip. Sip. Hmm… What do I want to be? I would ask myself this deep question every time my independently thinking Nana would say those words—though it would soon be muffled out of earshot as I indulged in yet more sugar.

So how did I get from there to here? That's another book, but I did have a telltale dream that warned me I would never "make it" in Hollywood if I didn't give up sugar. I guess that warning from my inner guidance wasn't strong enough for me to put down the white stuff. No, it took ample hair loss and the threat of balding at thirty-nine years of age to bring home the fact that my body was out of balance. Once sugar was out of the picture, I finally came into focus.

I am eternally grateful to share this information with you.

introduction

As this is a sugar-free, gluten-free baking cookbook, I have compiled traditional and nontraditonal recipes using familiar and not so familiar ingredients. The recognizable ingredients like raisins, dates, apples, almonds, flaxseeds, and buckwheat flour will give you a sense of groundedness when approaching a new sugar-free, gluten-free recipe for the first time. The foreign or exotic ingredients like stevia, agave, erythritol, xanthan gum, and quinoa flour are unfamiliar at first, I agree. I sure thought they were. But like friends, you will grow to love them in time and will above all appreciate them for their unique characteristics and individual qualities that make sugar-free, gluten-free baking and dehydrating even possible—and most of all, highly desireable.

Dehydrated recipes are included in the book because they are easy. Batters don't need to be perfectly measured or mixed. Also, the dehydrating method greatly reduces the occurrence of burnt baked goods. I bake weekly and I dehydrate monthly. I dehydrate less often because huge batches of cookies and crackers will last for weeks if stored in an airtight container. Dehydrating is a form of baking at low temperatures to preserve the nutrients and enzymes contained in whole foods. Because raw vegan desserts made in a dehydrator are nutrient and calorie dense, they aid in teaching the mind and body to eat sweets in proper proportions. You'll only want to eat one or two Hemp Ball Truffles and you will still be satisfied!

This cookbook also focuses on how to set up your pantry and get to know your new sugar-free, gluten-free alternative ingredients by choosing your first recipe, making a shopping list, finding a baking buddy if you want, and going on a field trip to your local health food store or supermarket that shelves organic whole foods and has a baking aisle with sugar-free, gluten-free alternatives. As this is a baking cookbook, I describe gluten-free baking techniques and raw, vegan food preparation techniques in the directions of each recipe. Also, you will find kitchen techniques and tips, plus suggestions for recipes to start with, during the introduction of each recipe chapter. If you are already experienced in the art of baking, you will only have to discover the new ingredients that substitute for sugar and flour and decide which brands you'll want to use. There are many brands of agave now, and erytritol, too.

When I first began my sugar-free, gluten-free journey, most of the product brands were not available. Now you will find most of the ingredients at Whole Foods Market. If you can't find an ingredient, have the grocery team leader put in a special order for you. Or, you can always save time, gas, and the ozone layer by purchasing ingredients online. If you are new to baking and are finding yourself beginning this process from scratch, know that the recipes are meant to be everyday desserts and snacks. Both novice and veteran bakers will experience for the first time the feel of a gluten-free dough and understand how to use spray oil on your spatula and hands for easy handling. Gluten-free dough is a sticky dough compared to a wheat dough. Once you get used to this, you will quickly make a batch of cookie dough every weekend and whip up pancake batter in your blender most mornings. When these basics are licked, you'll dare to try recipes like The Other White Loaf and make your own sandwich bread or you'll make Peaceful Pear and Pomegranate Tart with a pistachio crust for that special celebration. Are you ready?

Would you like to be free of sugar? And gluten, too? If so, what would being free of sugar and gluten look like, feel, and, most importantly, taste like? And if you do want to cook and bake sugar- and gluten-free, where do you go shopping? Just where do you begin? The answers to these questions are the keystones that gave me the inspiration, courage, and commitment it takes to go on the path of transformation, healing, and health through a sugar-free, gluten-free food practice. But it's easier than you think. With just one recipe like Fudge It, a 90-second gourmet truffle, I changed my life. You can too. This self-help cookbook offers a sugar-free, gluten-free cooking style and food philosophy that allows you to have your sweets and eat them too, and reap the benefits from this innovative, healthy, and delicious lifestyle.

First, sugar-free, gluten-free looks great on your body—inside and out. It increases the beauty and glow of your skin, hair, and face. By removing the inflammatory properties of white sugar and flour from your food plan and replacing them with sugar-free, gluten-free alternatives, not only can you reduce water retention, weight gain, premature wrinkles, poor digestion, a depressed immune system, and symptoms of overall aging, you can still have your sweets, without the guilt. Also, the most vital benefit we can gain from being sugar-free, gluten-free is keeping our blood sugar levels as even as possible, and therefore, our hormone levels as well. This is the very first transition you will notice. You will look and feel more beautiful, weigh less, and feel happier.

The second benefit of being sugar-free, gluten-free answers the question, "What does it feel like?" I just mentioned it feels happy, really happy. It also feels beautiful. Beyond happy and beautiful, it feels real. Really calm, peaceful, grounded, healthy, clear, steady, and nonaddictive. For me, being sugar-free, gluten-free feels absolutely free. Free to show up for myself, breathe deeply, and discover more of me, and that feels awesome.

It is also a miracle what I don't feel. I don't feel out of control around sugar, the urge to eat a bag of cookies is no more, and the compulsion around food is now a healthy impulse to nourish myself with sound and tasty nutrition that feeds my body and my spirit and still looks and tastes like a chocolate chip cookie. You just can't take away a kid's craving for a cookie (or mine, for that matter).

Now, the crucial question of taste. After eating one of my desserts, people say in amazement, "That has no sugar?" Truth is, it doesn't. No refined white sugar at all. The third and ultimate reward of cooking and eating sugar-free, gluten-free is the sweet and satisfying taste without the ill effects of sugar: headache, bloat, dull and blemished skin, spiked blood sugar levels, and hormonal imbalances. You have to taste it to believe it. Some of the recipes in this book are supersweet and some are slightly sweet. Try a recipe out and give yourself the taste-bud challenge. Not all taste buds are made the same. Most have been trained for years to enjoy all the wicked whites: sugar, salt, flour, and creamy butter. Mine have definitely transformed into desiring healthy and naturally sweet-tasting foods through the process of becoming free of sugar. White sugar now tastes like a chemical and not a food. Using natural sweeteners like agave, stevia, and erythritol tastes better to me than sugar, honey, and maple syrup, can replace the liquid component of sugar in baking, and can have either a low-glycemic index or no GI at all. How can that not taste great?

Now that you know you don't have to live without sweets and that the alternative ingredients to sugar and glutenous flours can be used to heal your body and satisfy your sweet tooth—where do you get the goods? And how do you begin?

Weekly planning and preparation with a menu and food-shopping list are your best tools for success. Once your list is hand, you can visit your local health food store or my website, www.kellykeough.com, for online ordering.

Getting your sugar-free, gluten-free pantry stocked is a breeze, making your first recipe is fun, and discovering the sweet truth—your true identity—with the support of a sugar-free, gluten-free food philosophy and practice is so satisfying. And that's because...the sweet truth is YOU!

the sweet truth

a sugar-free, gluten-free cooking style and food philosophy

The Sweet Truth is a breakthrough food practice that heals sugar and flour addiction, increases self-esteem, and allows you to have your sweets and eat them, too. "Great," you say. "But will I lose weight?" Definitely.

The magic key to health and beauty is to keep the blood sugar level even by not eating white sugar and gluten flour. Both are high in glucose and raise insulin levels in the blood, causing fat storage. Replace them with the tools of nature: agave, stevia, quinoa, and buckwheat.

Sugar and flour are highly allergenic and slow down digestion; if you are gluten intolerant, both may stop absorption of vitamins and minerals. Therefore, increase your nutrient-dense foods like seaweed and organic leafy greens as well. Increase digestive fires and stimulate metabolism and reduce inflammation with spices like cinnamon and turmeric. And cook! Cook! Cook!

Also, weigh and measure your meals along with the amount of stress you take in and give out. Pray that each meal is enough food and always know there will be another.

Most of all, still eat dessert without stimulating your compulsion for overeating! Sweetness is the essence of life and opens the gateway for you to experience your true identity. Meet your culinary destiny as I have met mine. It starts in the kitchen.

But above all, live and love your one and only own sweet truth.

my story, a little story...

"Terrible Two." That's the label with which we adults lovingly anoint a small person of 24 months who has hasn't quite figured out that there are other people on this planet besides themselves.

Only two and already terrible. Yet this is the name I gave myself at the tender age of 730 days as I stood barefoot on the cold, dark-spotted linoleum bathroom floor of my grandmother's house in western New York. It was my home away from home and the center of "Chiavetta's Barbeque Chicken and Catering Business," famous for taste. For me, it provided too much easy, backstage access to food. Down at my belly I stared, dressed in a yellow bikini, and said, "C'est terrible!" Well, I couldn't speak French yet, but if I could, that's what I would have said.

How can a child at the age of two understand the concept of "fat"? Call me an intuitive baby, but I did, and I knew. I was a chubby bubby. And I didn't like it. From that moment on, I hated myself and my body; never mind the yellow polka-dot bikini that only looks good on dolls.

I guess I could have blamed it all on the barbecue chicken that was available to me on a 24/7 basis, but let's face it: The truth is, it was the lemon-filled sheet cakes. Or was it the strawberry-filled cake with chocolate frosting? I'll eat cake over chicken any day. And that's what I did growing up in a Sicilian family with a catering business. I ate cake and lots of it! But I do blame my grandmother for putting me on the cake service line instead of the chicken when I worked for their catering business every summer since the age of fourteen. How else was I supposed to keep the spatula clean?

It's been forty years since then and then some...

a different story

Addicted to sugar? Who isn't? I can honestly say I was and I am not anymore. And I healed from this terrible disease through my sugar-free, gluten-free food practice. I didn't go without; I ate better than I ever have and had desserts without guilt. Did I lose weight? Yes, and for the first time in my life, without trying. I no longer diet, I plan food—or in other words, I have a food plan that satisfies my sweet tooth. Believe me, at first it was daunting and yet I dared myself to put myself back into balance. I was desperate to recover the third of my hair that had fallen out due to chronic emotional and nutritional stress. The message I gave myself was that I had to heal, not lose weight. And that's ultimately how I lost weight. I focused instead on being sugar-free and gluten-free. The same can happen to you. You can lose weight, look great, and have shiny, strong hair all with the Sweet Truth cooking style and food philosophy. Not a diet but a new practice: guilt-free sweet recipes, from breakfast to dessert, for radiant beauty and easy weight loss using diabetic-safe agave, stevia, and other natural foods that are low-glycemic sweeteners in conjunction with good fats, fiber, and protein to keep blood sugar levels balanced and properly fed.

Rooted in organic, whole foods and excluding all refined white sugar and gluten flour, the recipes in this self-help cookbook also use sweet fruits and vegetables, and gluten-free whole grains like quinoa, buckwheat, sorghum flour, and garbanzo bean flour. It's great for people on low-glycemic diets, those with type II diabetes, hypoglycemia, or celiac disease. I created this practice to regrow my hair and balance my hormonal system and was given so much more. I discovered more of who I am. By stripping away the sugar and flour, I uncovered more of me. Now, I love to wear bathing suits.

Low-carb diets are good for some people, but not for me and definitely not for you if you want to enjoy what life has to offer. And that is sweetness with a low-glycemic index and lots of nutrition. But that doesn't mean I go off and eat what I want whenever I want. I eat one-cup or half-cup servings or two cookies at a time because I believe a balanced body, mind, and spirit equal the trinity of beauty, truth, and clear perception of the self. And I think myself a queen.

Whether Marie Antoinette said it or not, "Let them eat cake!" is a command I am eagerly willing to obey. Why? Because I am the official, self-proclaimed Queen of Quinoa, I know how to eat cake and still lose the weight without the guilt because I bake with high protein, gluten-free quinoa flour. I even know how to answer the number one question posed by people starting off on a new and exotic food adventure, "What do I eat for breakfast?" The answer? Something sweet, delicious, and satiating with high protein and a low-glycemic index so you're not feeling deprived by 10:00 a.m.

Getting off sugar was the key for me in losing the first fifty pounds and eventually going gluten-free aided in the last twelve pounds. So if you want get off sugar and flour and yet are afraid to, then this cookbook is for you. I promise, you'll find a recipe that works for you and your family and still satisfies your sweet tooth.

planning

Start with one simple recipe like a dessert. Make a grocery list of the items you don't already have in your pantry. Plan a trip to your local natural food store, or shop online or at my website, www.kellykeough.com. There you will find alternative ingredients for sugar: agave, stevia, yacon, and erythritol. You'll also find wheat alternatives: all-purpose gluten-free flour and xanthan gum. You'll also want a few superfoods: goji berries, raw cacao powder, raw cacao nibs, and hempseeds.

I suggest starting with the recipe No Guilt Brownies. This recipe has very few alternative ingredients like stevia and xanthan gum and contains items probably already in your kitchen like eggs, cinnamon, and vanilla extract. It's also a dessert that looks, smells, and tastes familiar to everyone in the family, especially if they don't know that there's black beans and tahini in it. For this recipe you'll need the following ingredients to build your pantry:

AGAVE

COCONUT-DATE ROLLS OR MEDJOOL DATES

UNSWEETENED ALMOND MILK

BLACK BEANS, DRAINED

RAW TAHINI (NO SALT ADDED)

LIQUID STEVIA CHOCOLATE

ROASTED CAROB POWDER

ALL-PURPOSE GLUTEN-FREE FLOUR

GLUTEN-FREE BAKING POWDER

BAKING SODA

XANTHAN GUM

UNSWEETENED CAROB CHIPS

BRAZIL NUTS

✒ BAKING BUDDY

After the recipe is chosen and the grocery list is complete, round up a baking buddy to split the cost, consumption, and cleanup. Sugar-free, gluten-free baking or making raw vegan desserts is worth the time, money, and friendship. You'll not only strengthen your relationship with your baking buddy, but you'll start the process of turning food from a foe to a friend as well. It's a great plan.

preparation

Writing a grocery list and dreaming about what you are going to eat helps you to use your imagination. It's a lot of fun, especially when you know you are going to make and eat a guilt-free and satisfying dessert. Making a list helps me commit to my healing process on a weekly basis. Creative and committed consistency is the key to success of any practice. In this case, it's a sugar-free, gluten-free food practice. If I didn't heal my stress, remove sugar and flour from my food plan, and balance my system, I'd go bald. It was that simple. I was ready to commit. This health problem completely put me in the moment. I watched everything I put in my mouth. Within two weeks, people where commenting on my glowing skin and my effortless weight loss. I was changing my looks through food. I was also changing the way I felt about myself on the inside. This gave me the self-esteem and motivation to go forward. And eating desserts that healed me and satisfied my sweet tooth gave me the fascination and encouragement to stay disciplined and committed.

Now that you have a grocery list, the next step is to plan a three-hour block of time each week for baking, then have fun. Cooking in the kitchen like this will burn over four hundred calories. I look at it as an opportunity for exercise. It's also a time to infuse your own healing energy into your cooking and think positively about yourself. Instant therapy! That's what I call it and it only costs the price of food. I get many good ideas to solve problems when I am in the kitchen, and it's also my great escape from the pressures of living in Los Angeles and being away from my family and best friends in Massachusetts.

The relatively short time it takes to plan a grocery list that in three hours will turn out four sugar-free, gluten-free, satisfying recipes on a weekly basis is a very rewarding and grounding activity. It can be done with a best friend, with family members, or solo. Either way, planning and preparation yields success for an optimum healthy lifestyle that is enjoyable and tastes better than it ever did.

If I didn't cook, I'd lose my mind and gain lots of weight. Preparation through planning and cooking has given me the gift of the goddess—it has put me in touch with my deep creative resources and connection to myself and others by being able to nurture myself through my food practice. I love myself more for it. And it is all because of releasing (really surrendering) sugar and flour from my life. This last sentence brings me to the third and most powerful principle of all: PRAYER.

prayer

I just mentioned how cooking for people is a grounded and sensual show of love, and being loved in return, especially if the dish tastes amazing and is satisfying. And isn't this reminiscent of Mother? Mother is the one who fed us, or didn't feed us. As adults, Mother Earth feeds us now by growing food sources for us, and yes, she even grows sugar cane, but she also grows agave and stevia. Mother knows we need sweets. Sweet is a metaphor for love and love is what we all want and crave.

When I feel I don't get enough love, I tend to overeat—and this is where the praying comes in. Every time I eat I pray, "God, let this be enough food and let me know there will always be another meal." Sometimes for me, satisfying my sweet tooth with a no-guilt, sugar-free, gluten-free dessert is not enough. Intuiting the amount that is perfect for my body must be a part of my food practice. Let me repeat. This is a practice. Every meal is a new opportunity to be in alignment with my inner balance of beauty, truth, and perception. Since I was a compulsive overeater, I use a measuring cup. I believe in eating to satisfy, especially when beginning a new food plan. Then as your body loses weight and balances all its systems, you will need less food naturally. Ultimately you will come to know that you are loved. Always. It took me 42 years to figure that out. But even when I was in the dark about this, I diligently executed my food practice, I measured my food and found that because I wasn't eating sugar, I wasn't triggering my sugar addiction. I naturally began to eat suggested serving sizes like two small cookies for dessert.

Measuring is just as much a technical exercise as it is a spiritual exercise. Being aware of the amount of stress you are taking on is just as important as monitoring the amount of food you are taking in. Less stress is less opportunity to overeat. Here are some guidelines for measuring. At first, start out with the one-cup rule. One cup of grains, beans or lentils, sautéed veggies or root vegetable, or dessert. After three months, or when your body naturally tells you to cut back, go to three-quarters of a measuring cup and then to a half cup. Don't fret. When you have the last five to ten pounds to lose like me, it's enough food. That's what my body tells me. This is the reward or "fruit" of the practice—that your ability to use your body as an intuitive tool for healing becomes more apparent.

Releasing sugar and gluten flour from your system, along with other toxins, will give you the ability to be present in your body and listen to its wisdom. Couple this with yoga, meditation, exercise you love, and a sugar-free, gluten-free, nutrient-dense food practice and you are on your way to freedom, to dream like you never did before. Therefore, praying becomes second nature. Remember to do it at each meal. What will start to happen is your body will tell you how much to measure, what ingredients are good for you, and what you're allergic to even before you eat. Actually, your body already does this. Once you start the practice, you will start to listen. And isn't that what you want God to do when you pray?

food as tools of nature

Now that you know the tips, here are the tools. On the pages that follow are lists of alternative foods or tools I use on a consistent basis. Starting with the sugar-free pantry items like agave and stevia, these sugar-free alternatives vary in glycemic index, calories, and carbohydrates. For me sugar-free does not mean calorie- and carb-free. For this cookbook, it means low-glycemic, or no glycemic, and with low carbs or no carbs that when combined in my recipes with high fiber, protein, and good fats break down slowly in the body. And when you are ready, desserts warrant portion control. Portion control will naturally happen at a point once processed sugar and flour is omitted from your food plan. This especially occurs when you cook for yourself on a weekly basis. In order to do this, you must execute the planning and preparation tools.

These essential planning and preparation tools include: a list of the pantry staples, a shopping list, sample menus, explanations on the sugar-free, gluten-free alternative ingredients and superfoods, and the recipes.

For me, I intend to use food as tool, for the healing properties of nature, and for their holistic benefits. You can use these food tools just for great tasting recipes. The tools of nature are the backbone to the success of practicing the Sweet Truth. These tools of nature also include fresh, organic whole fruits and vegetables, herbs, and spices.

Using food as a building block balanced my system by boosting vitality, increasing metabolism, increasing digestion and absorption, tuning the hormonal system, evening out mood and mental outlook, and detoxifying and warding off free radicals which leave the body, mind, and spirit clear and free. I couldn't help but raise my self-esteem. And you can too. Here's to your culinary destiny!

the pantry

setting up your sugar-free pantry

Sugar-free ingredients and recipes in this cookbook do not mean carbohydrate free, but they do mean free of processed white sugar, cane juice, honey, maple syrup, corn syrup, high fructose corn syrup, molasses, and brown sugar, all of which have a high-glycemic index, or above fifty. In the recipes that follow, you will use a new list of sugar-free ingredients as alternatives to white sugar and other high-glycemic sweeteners. I describe what a glycemic index is and how it affects your blood sugar in the next section. Agave, which looks and tastes like a sweet syrup and can be used to substitute white sugar, is the most common sugar alternative you will see at grocery stores across the country in the baking aisle. I describe agave in detail below. You'll discover that I also use yacon syrup, coconut sugar, and sometimes dates to replace molasses and brown sugar—the main ingredients found in regular-sugared baked goods, which are necessary to retain moisture and give color and caramelization to baked products.

Ingredients like agave, yacon, and coconut sugar have low-glycemic indexes of fifty or below. Yet these above mentioned all-natural sweeteners do have calories, so in my recipe formulations I have combined them with other sweeteners that have a zero-glycemic index and have no or very few calories and are all-natural, coming from fruits, vegetables, or herbs. These new ingredients include stevia, a green-leafed herb from Paraguay. Then there is erythritol, a fermented polyol or sugar alcohol, which is the best choice out of all the polyols for its ease on the digestive system. Also there are isoliogofructose or inulin, which is fiber from chicory and is combined with erythritol in a brand of sugar alternative called Swerve.

The most important sugar-free baking technique to know is that not just one sugar-free alternative replaces white sugar or brown sugar. Processed white sugar has its own unique flavor and note. In most of the recipes, you will find that I use an average of three different alternatives to capture the taste, the note, and the baking qualities found in sugar. For example, in a chocolate chip cookie recipe that calls for white sugar and brown sugar, I use agave, stevia, and erythritol. Agave is used for moisture and sweetness as well as caramelization. Stevia is used for only sweetness and therefore can be eliminiated. Erythritol is used for sweetness and volume in the recipe. Building your sugar-free pantry is like adding a new network of friends; at first they seem unfamiliar, but over time, they will surprise you with new opportunities to grow and develop yourself in ways you never knew existed.

These sugar alternatives seem exotic, but they can be found at your local Whole Foods Market and health food store in the nutrition section or baking aisle. You can also order them online and find their websites listed in the ingredient lists in Setting Up Your Pantry sections of this chapter.

My main sweetener is agave nectar. Organic light and dark, most agave syrups are made from the succulent blue weber agave, a cactus like plant grown in Mexico. Agave is a very affordable, super-healthy sugar alternative and is found in most health food stores. It replaces honey and is used in my baking as a liquid sugar. The blue weber agave plant makes many products, the most popular of which is tequila, but that's only if the agave plant is grown in the Jalisco region of Mexico. The long 10- to 12-foot leaves of the agave are cut off and the *pina*, the bottom stem of the plant that is attached to the root but above ground, is harvested. The juice from the *pina* is squeezed out and through a cooking process made into nectar or honey.

It's important to know that the blue weber agave is the only agave plant to produce a nectar that is diabetic safe with a low-glycemic index, usually under fifty. Other species of agave plants may have different fructose levels and not be beneficial for people who desire to watch their sugar intake. Organic blue weber agave grows abundantly in many regions of Mexico, not just in Jalisco. Legend has it that there was a goddess, Mayahuel, who was a trickster. Another ruling god did not approve of her flirtatious ways, chopped off her head, and cut her into tiny pieces. The farmers and people of the town loved Mayahuel so much, they buried her body all over the land. Mayahuel resurrected herself through the great love of the people and grew back as an abundant succulent, agave. Now everyone can taste her fruits. There are other natural sweeteners like stevia that have a zero-glycemic index.

Liquid and powdered stevia is produced by a green-leafed plant from Paraguay, and oligofructose and erythritol, trademarked as Zeratol, is made from fruit and vegetable fiber. These are my main sugar-free sweeteners and they are always stocked in my pantry.

These sweeteners are all-natural and made with no chemicals. What I don't use—natural or not—is high fructose corn syrup, fructose crystals, maple syrup, corn syrup, turbinado, brown rice syrup, honey, molasses, organic cane or brown sugar, xylitol, sorbitol, manitol, Splenda, or NutraSweet. Those sweeteners make me bloated, gain weight, compulsively eat more sugar, and give me diarrhea and headaches.

Agave and stevia are not fake sugars like Splenda or NutraSweet. I carefully chose the best, all-natural and organic sweeteners I could find that have no glycemic index at all like stevia or a very low glycemic index like agave to keep my body and sugar cravings in balance.

And one last mention on salt in my recipes: In traditional baking, salt is used as an ingredient to bring out the sweetness in processed white sugar. Because many of the alternative ingredients I use, like stevia and erythritol, are blended together for a whole bodied sweetness and are already many times sweeter than white sugar, salt is not a necessary ingredient. You will find salt used sparingly, or not at all, in recipes throughout the cookbook for this reason.

✑ WHAT IS A GLYCEMIC INDEX?

All carbohydrate foods like bread, cookies, yams, carrots, or quinoa are not created equal. They each affect my body differently. If I eat a yam, I feel great and have no ill side effects. If I eat an Oreo cookie, I want to eat ten more (even though I don't anymore), but even after one, I feel the ill effects of a sharp rise in my blood sugar. This is especially true now that I have been free of sugar for over three years.

According to the University of Sydney, the glycemic index (or GI) describes this difference in food by ranking carbohydrates according to their effect on our blood glucose levels. Choosing low GI carbs—the ones that produce only small fluctuations in our blood glucose and insulin levels and have a GI of fifty or below—is the secret to my long-term health, losing weight and keeping it off, looking young, reducing pain in my body, reducing wrinkles, and slowing the aging process, as well as protecting my most treasured organ, my heart. Low GI foods helped heal my body and now I want to keep myself young, healthy, beautiful, and in balance. This is important to me because I would like to have a baby in a few years.

I suffered from childhood obesity. Now childhood obesity and diabetes is a U.S. epidemic. The great news is that mothers can now use agave and stevia to make diabetic-safe treats that will help aid in the battle of these childhood diseases. I wish my mother had known how to make a sugar-free, gluten-free chocolate chip cookie when I was a kid. Because if she did, she would have treated me with a happy confection containing a very low glycemic index, high fiber, high protein, and good fat so my body could have maintained health and balance from head to toe. These are some of the benefits of eating low-GI desserts.

definition of glycemic index

Glycemic Index (GI): The glycemic index is a dietary index that's used to rank carbohydrate-based foods. For the sake of this book, I focus on the glycemic index of the sweeteners I use like agave, stevia, and zeratol. The glycemic index predicts the rate at which the ingested food will increase blood sugar levels. It ranks carbohydrates from 0 to 100 based on how fast they affect the level of glucose in the bloodstream (commonly referred to as the "blood sugar" level). Glucose, or sugar, has a GI of 100, meaning it enters the bloodstream immediately; this is the reference point against which other foods are compared, like white bread with a GI of 80, Splenda 80, agave 11–19, and stevia 0 (see chart on page 183).

What does all this mean? I was desperate to have my sweets and eat them, too, so I created recipes that satisfy my sweet tooth, are made with organic whole grains, fruits, vegetables, and gluten-free flours—and therefore are high in fiber. Along with that I add good fats, high protein, and low-glycemic or zero glycemic sweeteners like stevia and agave. When I switched to this type of food plan, I lost weight without trying and ate more desserts per week than I ever did my entire life. That's because this combination of high fiber and protein coupled with good fats and low-glycemic sweeteners kept my blood sugar steady and therefore didn't make me gain weight.

Of course, I exercise almost every day and have since I was 19 years old. Even today I do the movement I love most: ballet, salsa, yoga, and surfing. I love ballet and yoga for the discipline and salsa and surfing for the cute men.

Even though you won't find white sugar or flour in my kitchen today, I didn't get there overnight. Start slowly and see what appeals to you first. It may all seem exotic, but if you have an illness like diabetes and/or obesity, you may just be inspired to try agave at the very least (and agave is very affordable). Here's a list of my sugar-free, alternative sweeteners. The best advice I can give you is to check out this list and then look at my top 15 ingredients.

～ SUGAR-FREE ALTERNATIVES

The following ingredients can be found at Whole Foods Market or your local health food store. If you don't have easy access to these stores, you can find links to all the products I use on my website, www.kellykeough.com.

agave, dark

Comes organic and is made from the blue weber agave cactuslike plant grown in Mexico. The blue weber agave is the same plant from which tequila is made. Agave is high in fructose rather than glucose, which allows it to be absorbed slowly into the blood stream, avoiding the "rush" often associated with refined sugar. Agave is 50 percent sweeter than white table sugar and is my replacement for honey. Dark agave is cooked a longer time than light agave, has more minerals, and has a GI of about 11. It's also safe for diabetics. Use 1 to 2 teaspoons in a serving.

agave, light

Like its darker sibling, light agave comes from the blue weber agave plant grown in Mexico. Light agave is cooked for the least amount of time, has a GI of 19, and is safe for diabetics. Use 1 to 2 teaspoons in a serving.

WWW.KELLYKEOUGH.COM

cacao, raw—nibs and powder

Raw cacao is chocolate in its natural form: a nib, shelled from its pod. Nibs come roasted or raw and are available as organic. Both have a very bitter taste, but the raw nibs are a great way to get a hit of chocolate without any extra added sugar or emulsifiers. Raw cacao is high in magnesium and aids digestion.

WWW.NAVITASNATURALS.COM

carob chips, dairy-free

Made from carob powder and sweetened with barley malt, these chips contain no whey or milk, but they are definitely not gluten-free.

carob chips, unsweetened

Made from carob powder, nonfat milk, whey powder, palm kernel oil, and soy lecithin, so they contain dairy but no added sugar. They often take the place of chocolate chips in my recipes to avoid extra sugar. Also, you must check the label; Sunspire carob chips do not guarantee that they are gluten-free. Carob chips don't melt well, but are great in cookies, muffins, scones, or just as a quick snack.

carob powder—raw or roasted

A powder or fine flour ground from the carob pod or locust bean. It is a natural sweetener, low in fat, has no caffeine, and is a digestive aid. Its dark brown color and flavor substitutes for chocolate because it has a cocoalike taste but lacks the bitterness of chocolate. The powder is available in two forms: raw carob powder for a milk chocolate flavor or substitute, and roasted carob powder for dark chocolate. I prefer roasted carob for all my recipes. It keeps better, as raw carob tends to clump up even when stored in an airtight container.

chocolate chips, gluten-free substitute

Instead of using grain-sweetened chocolate chips, in a double boiler, melt 3 ounces of 99 percent dark unsweetened baking chocolate with 1 tablespoon light agave and 1 dropper liquid stevia. Whisk in 1 tablespoon unsweetened almond milk. Spread chocolate on baking sheet covered with wax paper. Chill 30 minutes. Break into pieces and use as chips.

chocolate chips, grain-sweetened

Chocolate chips sweetened with malted barley and corn but no white sugar like traditional chocolate chips. They are not gluten-free. I sometimes use them with unsweetened carob chips when melting chocolate because carob chips alone don't melt smoothly.

cocoa baking bars, unsweetened

Many baking bars have added sugar, so look for one that is 99 percent cocoa. I use Scharffen Berger 99 percent unsweetened baking cocoa bars. They melt well and have a rich dark-chocolate flavor.

cocoa powder, unsweetened

Made from roasted cocoa nibs. I like to use Valrhona 100 percent cocoa powder. It's easy to find and blends well with roasted carob powder. This is a great health tip for adding natural sweetness to your baked goods while cutting down on the caffeine.

coconut sugar (palm sugar)

A product from the Philippines, this organic sweetener is made from evaporated coconut sap or sweet toddy. It looks like brown sugar and acts like brown sugar in baking by holding in moisture. The glycemic index is 35, which is a lower GI than some agave syrups.

WWW.NAVITASNATURALS.COM

NATURESBLESSINGS.COM.PH

dried fruit

Dates, coconut-date rolls, raisins, mulberries, golden berries, and figs are all found in my pantry, especially during holiday time. Even though dried fruit is a high-glycemic food, when it is combined with whole grains, agave, stevia, fiber, and good fats, the digestion and absorption of the carbohydrates is slower than usual and will not adversely affect blood sugar.

WWW.NAVITASNATURALS.COM

goji berries

Grown primarily in China, the goji berry is a not-so-sweet dried red berry known for its high nutritional value: high in vitamin C and amino acids, antioxidants, and medicinal qualities for a healthy heart. The dried goji berries can be added to granola, trail mix, and smoothies.

WWW.NAVITASNATURALS.COM

stevia extract

Made from the *Stevia rebaudina* green-leafed plant from Paraguay. The benefits of stevia are that it is diabetic safe, calorie free, three hundred times sweeter than sugar, and doesn't adversely affect blood sugar. It is also nontoxic, inhibits formation of cavities and plaque, contains no artificial ingredients, and has a zero glycemic index. Comes in a very concentrated powdered form and is not recommended for baking, only for sweetening drinks. This is the same as Stevia Plus Powder, minus the FOS.

stevia, liquid drops

As a fine white powder, it is known as stevioside, but here the stevia is in liquid form and much easier to use in drinks and baking. It can come flavored with all-natural flavoring and no alcohol. My top pantry flavors are Vanilla Crème, Dark Chocolate, Lemon Drops, Cinnamon, and Grape. The benefit of liquid stevia is that it mixes best in drinks and wet baking mixtures. Believe it or not, sugar is considered a wet ingredient in baking, and liquid stevia is my sugar replacement, too. I carry Vanilla Crème in my pocketbook at all times and use it at the coffee shop. Another benefit is that you can buy an unflavored liquid stevia and add your own extracts for flavor.

WWW.WISDOMNATURALBRANDS.COM

stevia plus powder

As a fine white powder, it is known as stevioside, but here it is mixed with an FOS, fructooligosaccharide, for more volume. This makes Stevia Plus Powder easier to measure for baking. Stevia Plus Powder is my replacement for sugar especially when combined with agave. Comes in packets for easy travel or in small bulk containers for your pantry.

WWW.WISDOMNATURALBRANDS.COM

swerve and zsweet

Made from fruit and vegetable fiber, erythritol is the only polyol or sugar alcohol that is fermented. It is easily digested and can be organic. It works best as a table sugar. Adding erythritol to tea, smoothies, yogurt, cereal, and fresh fruit is the best choice for using this natural sweetener. ZSweet is a common brand. Oligofructose is inulin from chicory and is combined with erythritol in a product called Swerve. This combination of sugar substitutes of erythritol and oligofructose is the best for baking because Swerve tastes the most like sugar and is also available in a confectioners' style for making frosting and icing. Because neither erythritol or oligofructose hold in the moisture in baked goods, an oil, such as extra-virgin coconut oil or grapeseed oil, along with agave, can be used in recipes to add moistness. Both Swerve and ZSweet have a zero glycemic index and four grams erythritol carbohydrate grams per serving.

WWW.ZSWEET.COM

WWW.SWERVESWEETENER.COM

truvia

Made from fruit and vegetable fiber, erythritol is the only polyol or sugar alcohol that is fermented. It is easily digested and can be organic. It works best as a table sugar. Adding erythritol to tea, smoothies, yogurt, cereal, and fruit is the best choice in using this natural sweetener. Rebiana is a derivative of the stevia plant and is the sweetest part extracted from the leaf. The combination of rebiana and erythritol can be found in a table sugar product called Truvia and is best used in tea, smoothies, yogurt, cereal, and on fresh fruit.

WWW.TRUVIA.COM

yacon—slices, powder, syrup

Scientifically known as *Smallanthus sonchifolius*, yacon is a root vegetable from Peru. Yacon roots can be eaten raw and have a pleasant sweetness that comes in part from fructans, carbohydrates that are not metabolized by the human body and therefore can be safely consumed by diabetics. You can buy yacon slices, powder, or syrup, which are available organic, online or at your health food store. Powder is sometimes difficult to find, but slices are usually available, especially online, so I grind the slices into a powder in my high-powered blender.

WWW.NAVITASNATURALS.COM

❧ HERBS AND SPICES

I recognized the real power of sweet and savory spices and herbs when I went sugar-free and gluten-free and that's because I had to make everything myself. Using more spices and herbs when I needed to satisfy my taste buds without the extra carbs, calories, sodium, and bad fats was paramount to my consistent dedication and love for self-nurture in the kitchen.

Having a "diet mentality" cannot only make me feel deprived, it does deprive me and usually leads to malnutrition and bad-tasting food devoid of the natural benefits of spices and fresh herbs.

It was when I took my health into my own hands and decided to heal myself through food that I greatly expanded my spice and herb cabinet. Always thinking I had to lose weight made food taste weak and boring, especially if the only methods I used were my George Foreman grill for meats and a steamer for vegetables.

In fact, changing from a diet mentality to a self-nurturing outlook has me eating healthy and gourmet every day. I found that completely satisfying my taste buds is the key to balanced eating and sticking to a healthy food plan.

The main spices that I have within reach at all times are cinnamon, turmeric, ginger, cayenne, nutmeg, pumpkin pie spice, cardamom, clove, apple pie spice, allspice, fennel, garam masala, curry, and Celtic sea salt. I use these spices for their digestive, anti-inflammatory, and metabolism-raising benefits.

Think of cinnamon as an everyday spice and sweetener. Cinnamon is a spice I buy in bulk and have at least once a day in a smoothie, cooked cereal, granola, or apple dessert. Cinnamon is a sweet spice and a metabolism spice, increasing circulation. Not only do I use cinnamon for its satisfying and sweet taste, I use it as an energy elixir when combined with dates and carob in many of my recipes. It has been noted that cinnamon may significantly help people with type II diabetes to improve their ability to respond to insulin and help them normalize their blood sugar levels.

Use turmeric because of its anti-inflammatory properties, which produce soft skin and fewer wrinkles. Turmeric, like many other spices, is an antioxidant, which means it stabilizes unstable oxygen molecules, better known as free radicals. Many of the spices I listed above are used in Ayurvedic healing.

setting up your gluten-free pantry

Gluten-free baking means that all of the ingredients are free of gluten with the exception of grain-sweetened chocolate chips, for which I give a gluten-free note and substitution in each recipe. I eliminated gluten from my food plan not because I have celiac disease, but because I wanted better digestion and absorption of nutrients; I wanted to lose weight and heal my sugar cravings; and I wanted to stop my hair from falling out and to start growing it back. I wanted to rid myself of the glutenous grains that contain the gooey protein strand that gives baked goods their height and form. Eliminating wheat, barley, rye, spelt, and kamut increased my digestive health and allowed me to slim down effortlessly, so my efforts shifted to getting back into the kitchen and cooking.

In my sugar-free, gluten-free food practice and recipes, I use gluten-free grains and flours. Oats can be used if they are labeled as gluten-free oats that have been grown in designated oat fields so as to ensure no crossbreeding with any nearby wheat fields. Yet some celiacs cannot tolerate even gluten-free oats and should check with their doctor. There are recipes in this book that call for gluten-free oats. By eliminating glutenous grains and flours like wheat flour, pasta, and couscous, I found that not only do I have better digestion, less bloating, and feel pain-free with less inflammation in my body, I experienced firsthand that I look and feel the best I ever have.

Yet wheat-free does not mean gluten-free. Wheat-free products may still contain other glutenous grains and flours like rye, barley, spelt, kamut, and oats. The majority of the recipes in this cookbook use gluten-free grains and are gluten-free recipes, except in certain recipes where I use oats, grain-sweetened chocolate chips, or almond milk, which is usually sweetened with brown rice syrup made from malted barley. To substitute oats, use a double amount of puffed brown rice; for any prepared milk alternative, like almond milk that has been sweetened with brown rice syrup or malted barley, use unsweetened almond milk or soy milk. For carob chips, check to see that they are unsweetened and completely guaranteed by the manufacturer to be gluten-free.

I have benefited tremendously from eliminating gluten from my food plan by using gluten-free whole grains and flours and at the same time I have never felt like I have to live without.

WHAT IS CELIAC DISEASE AND WHAT DOES GLUTEN-INTOLERANT MEAN?

People who have celiac disease or have been found to be gluten-intolerant have to be careful of all the food and processed food products they consume. Once diagnosed, they have to check with their doctors and get a list of gluten-free foods they can eat and then they may be able to add certain grains back into their food plans one at a time. In extreme cases, some of these grains may be millet, buckwheat, or even quinoa, which are considered gluten-free.

According to the Celiac Disease Foundation, celiac disease is defined as a chronic digestive disorder found in individuals that are genetically susceptible; the disease is possibly passed on from parent to child. The digestive damage happens in the small intestine where gluten found in products containing wheat, rye, barley, and oats causes a toxic reaction that prevents the nutrients in food from being properly absorbed.

Surprisingly, the following foods contain hidden gluten: dairy-free milks sweetened with brown rice syrup made from malted barley; soups; marinades; soy sauce made from wheat; imitation seafood; and anything made with modified food starch, malt flavoring, and dextrin (usually derived from corn but may be from wheat).

❧ HOW EASY IS IT TO GO GLUTEN-FREE, OR AT LEAST WHEAT-FREE?

If you have to have breads, cereals, and baked goods in your food plan (and who doesn't?), then you can find gluten-free and wheat-free products premade in your health food store. The catch is that they are not sugar-free. That's why this cookbook was born and why I make everything from scratch. My sugar-free, gluten-free recipes assure me that I know what I am eating and that I am taking care of my body, mind, and spirit. Just the process of making one sugar-free, gluten-free dessert like Fudge It serves as my tool for increasing my self-esteem and sugar-free satisfaction though self-nurture. The most important part of this formula is that it is my path to abstinence from the compulsive overeating of sugar and flour.

❧ ALTERNATIVE FLOUR INGREDIENTS FOR BAKING

This section lists the categories of baked goods in this cookbook and the alternative gluten-free flours used in the recipes to replace gluten flours such as white-wheat flour, whole-wheat flour, barley, rye, spelt, and oats that are not specifically marked on the label as "gluten-free." This cookbook calls for gluten-free oats. It is important to know that even though old-fashioned rolled oats and steel cut oats can be marked as "gluten-free" on the label, they may not be suitable for some people who have a gluten intolerance, especially people with celiac. Oats marked as "gluten-free" have been grown in special fields located a safe distance away from wheat fields and processed in designated gluten-free facilities.

The Alternative Flour Ingredients for Baking list (page 186) can be used if you don't have the exact flour ingredients on hand for a recipe and would like to use a different gluten-free flour or combination of gluten-free flours. This chart is also helpful if you have your own recipe that you want to transpose, and you would like to substitute white flour with a gluten-free flour. When transposing your own recipes, keep it simple. Switch out exact measurements of wheat flour with an all-purpose gluten-free flour. For example, if you are transposing a family recipe for chocolate chip cookies that calls for 2½ cups of white flour, substitute it with 2½ cups of an all-purpose gluten-free flour and add a teaspoon of xanthan gum. Xanthan gum is made from plant cellulose by extracting the vegetable fibers in corn or cabbage; it is vegan and is used in baking to hold gluten-free flours together.

The best all-purpose gluten-free flour is a combination of fava bean flour, garbanzo bean flour, potato starch, tapioca starch, and white sorghum flour. Bob's Red Mill All-Purpose Gluten-Free Flour uses this combination of flours and does not add extra leavening ingredients like baking soda and baking powder. This type of all-purpose flour is recommended for the recipes in this cookbook. I also recommend this all-purpose gluten-free flour because it does not contain brown rice flour, which has a grainy texture and can make baked goods fall apart easily even when combined with xanthan gum.

Gluten-free flour means free of gluten, but it does not mean free of calories and carbohydrates, nor does it suggest that it is a low-calorie food. Nor does gluten-free mean that prepared, store-bought products made from gluten-free flours are low-glycemic foods. Because of this, you must check labels and take note if the product made with gluten-free ingredients is also made with low-glycemic sweeteners and not cane sugar. Most of the time, this is not the case. This is the main reason why I created this sugar-free and gluten-free cookbook.

Many of the alternative flours used in this cookbook have a medium glycemic index and are high in protein like quinoa flour and chickpea (or garbanzo) flour. These types of flours are used many times in my nontraditional recipes, like No Guilt Brownies, containing black beans and tahini, which are wholesome snacks that can be made weekly. Using gluten-free flours and combining them with good fats, protein, and zero-calorie sweeteners lessens the glycemic load.

Also note that the intention of using gluten-free flours and gluten-free ingredients for this cookbook is to eliminate gluten for specific reasons of gluten intolerance or simple choices not to eat gluten. I recommend that all the recipes in this cookbook, including sweets, fruit desserts, snacks, and baked goods using alternative low-glycemic sweeteners and gluten-free flours, be portion controlled.

Other alternative flours like cornstarch, arrowroot, and white rice flour have high-glycemic indexes, especially potato flour. These high-glycemic, gluten-free flours are used only when needed in traditional recipes whose recipes call for a flaky texture or ability to rise, like piecrusts, cutout cookies, and white bread. I suggest that if you are watching your calorie and carbohydrate intakes, these types of recipes can be made for holidays, birthdays, and special occasions.

A Note on Allergy-free Baking: Although there are many recipes for baked sweets in this cookbook that use alternative ingredients to replace common food allergens, the best recipes for allergy-free baking are the raw, vegan recipes that replace butter with a whole apple or fruit, sugar with alternative sweeteners, eggs with soaked golden flaxseeds, and sprouted buckwheat for the flour. This way all sugar, dairy, eggs, nuts, corn, soy, and gluten flours are eliminated. These types of recipes use a dehydrator. Examples include allergy-free chocolate chip cookies, hemp protein bars, and oatmeal wheels using gluten-free oats and substituting Brazil nuts or pumpkin seeds for macadamia nuts if the recipe is accommodating a nut allergy (Brazil nuts are considered a seed).

WHEAT-FREE AND GLUTEN-FREE FLOURS

The following ingredients can be found at Whole Foods Market or your local health food store. If you don't have easy access to these stores, you can find links to all the products I use on my website, www.kellykeough.com.

agar agar flakes

Used to make kantens, agar agar flakes acts like gelatin but is completely vegan. A clear-looking, tasteless seaweed, it is found in the Asian aisle next to the sea vegetables at Whole Foods Market or your local health food store.

all-purpose gluten-free flour

An all-purpose baking flour made from garbanzo bean flour, potato starch, tapioca starch, white sorghum flour, and fava bean flour. This dry flour mix is prepared without added leavening ingredients like gluten-free baking powder, baking soda, and xanthan gum. For all the recipes in this cookbook, use an all-purpose gluten-free baking flour and add leavening ingredients.

WWW.BOBSREDMILL.COM

almond meal

Ground into flour from whole, sweet nuts. Can be used in combination with other flours and is used in breads, cakes, and pastries.

arrowroot

This starch, extracted from the rhizomes of the arrowroot plant, is used as a thickener and blends well with gluten-free flours. Interchangeable with cornstarch.

baking powder, gluten-free

Made from baking soda and cream of tartar and essential to a completely gluten-free baked good. Gluten-free baking powder can be bought at your local grocery store.

buckwheat flour

Buckwheat, related to rhubarb, is an herb, not a grain. It has a triangular-shaped seed and black shell, and is used whole in groat form or toasted groat form, can be cracked, or is ground into flour.

chia seed and combos with rice and flaxseed

Comes as a seed or is sprouted and blended into a flour that can be used in dehydrator breads, crackers, and cookies. Chia is one of the highest vegan sources of omega-3. Chia is also combined with rice and flaxseed to be used as a flour substitute in baking or can be added to raw recipes and smoothies for fiber, protein, and essential fatty acids.

WWW.NAVITASNATURALS.COM

cornmeal

Maize, a cereal plant native to the Americas. Kernels are largest of cereal seeds. Six major types are dent, flint, flour, sweet, pop, and pod corns. Cornmeal is used whole or processed into a multitude of products including sweeteners, flours, and oils.

cornstarch

Thickener derived from corn.

flaxseed and flaxseed meal

Seed of ancient medicinal herb with a nutty flavor. Can be used whole, toasted or sprouted; can be ground into meal; or is pressed into oil. High in fiber.

hazelnut meal

Ground from hazelnuts and may be blended with other flours or used to substitute for almond meal.

maca and roasted maca

A nourishing, yellow-colored root vegetable from the Andes Mountains of Peru, it is ground into a powder and can be used as a partial flour substitute in any recipe calling for gluten-free flour. Maca has a malt taste and blends well with carob and raw cacao powder to make a chocolate-malt flavor. The benefits of maca include better hormonal health, increased libido, and improved athletic performance. Maca also comes roasted, tastes like coffee, and has a dark brown color.

WWW.NAVITASNATURALS.COM

WWW.MACAMAGIC.COM

WWW.HEALTHYWISEORGANICS.COM

quinoa flour

Seed of ancient cereal grain of Peru, related to amaranth. Mild, nutty flavor. Versatile; can be substituted for any grain. Can be used whole as a grain and as a hot cereal or can be ground into flour. Adds moisture to baked goods.

kuzu

A Japanese root starch used as a thickener that can replace tapioca or cornstarch. Can be found in the Asian aisle next to the sea vegetables at Whole Foods Market or your local health food store.

polenta

Cooked corn. Comes either dry or wet in a ready-to-use package.

potato flour

Commercially ground from the whole potato, used as a thickener. Retains potato flavor. It looks and feels grainy and is a heavier flour than potato starch.

potato starch

Commercially prepared from cooked potatoes that are washed of all fibers until only the starch remains. Has the same consistency as tapioca and cornstarch. Not the same as potato flour.

protein powder, hemp

Comes organic and is made with hempseeds. Hemp contains protein, fiber, and omega-3, -6, and -9 fats. It is a great alternative to whey protein powder. Hemp protein powder can supply any diet with a vegetarian source of essential fatty acids, antioxidants, vitamins, minerals, fiber, chlorophyll, and a complete, balanced gluten-free source of the essential amino acids.

WWW.MANITOBAHARVEST.COM
NUTIVA.COM

protein powder, rice

Gluten-free and an alternative to soy, this protein powder is made from ground brown rice. Rice protein is derived by carefully isolating the protein from brown rice. It is a complete protein containing all essential and nonessential amino acids. Rice protein is hypoallergenic, which makes it suitable for everyone.

protein powder, whey and lactose-free whey

Whey protein is made from milk and is a common protein supplement. It contains nonessential and essential amino acids, as well as branch chain amino acids (BCAA). Amino acids are the building blocks of protein. The body does not make essential amino acids, therefore they must be obtained through diet. Nonessential amino acids can be synthesized by the body. Whey protein is not appropriate for those who are lactose intolerant, but a lactose-free version is available.

rice flour, brown

Ground form of brown rice with a nutty taste.

rice flour, white

Ground form of rice that is gluten-free and nonallergenic. This is the best flour to use when spray-oiling and flouring your baking pans and rolling out cookie and pizza dough.

sorghum flour, sweet

Drought-tolerant cereal grain used primarily as a flour or sweet syrup. Certified food-grade white sorghum has been specially developed for the food industry.

tapioca starch

Starchy substance extracted from the root of the cassava plant. Tapioca flour is used mainly in puddings as a thickener, especially in fruit dishes because it produces a clear gel.

xanthan gum

Used as a stabilizer, emulsifier, and thickener, and holds gluten-free baked goods together. It is also used as a thickener in fruit juices, as well as in the formation of various low-calorie foods. It is gluten-free, should be used with other gluten-free flours, and is made from vegetable cellulose.

WWW.BOBSREDMILL.COM

GLUTEN-FREE WHOLE GRAINS

brown rice

The whole grain of rice, from which the germ and outer layers containing the bran have not been removed. Unpolished rice.

buckwheat groats

Buckwheat is an amazing whole food. It comes in groats, or small triangular seeds. I buy my buckwheat in bulk and use it in my pancakes, muffins, cereals, breakfast breads, and candy. Like quinoa, it is high in protein and contains eight essential amino acids (eight proteins that the body cannot manufacture). Great news for vegetarians, but the best part about buckwheat is the fiber.

To me, as a so-called grain, nothing can compare. I say so-called because it is not a grain but, botanically speaking, a fruit and cousin to the rhubarb plant. Its digestibility and elimination properties without irritation to the digestive system are superior to any bran or oat product I've tried. For people who struggle with wheat allergies or gluten-intolerance, buckwheat is ideal. It has plenty of protein, B vitamins, and is rich in phosphorus, potassium, iron, and calcium. For me it aids in keeping my metabolism steady with no empty carb calories. This is a key factor in creating a steady blood sugar balance and aids in easy weight loss. Other known health benefits of buckwheat are that it may lower blood glucose and cholesterol, prevent fat accumulation, and promote safe and regular bowel movements. This information saved my life.

It also contains rutin, vitamin P, and choline. Rutin is a powerful bioflavonoid and is found in great quantities in buckwheat. Oddly, it is not found in other grains (rice, wheat, etc.) or even in beans! Rutin strengthens capillaries and aids against hardening of the arteries and high blood pressure. Vitamin P increases capillary strength and also functions to help absorb Vitamin C. And choline plays an important role in metabolism. It lowers blood pressure and hinders the deposit of fat in the liver. Good for people who drink a lot of sugar, namely beer!

kashi (toasted buckwheat groats)

When the triangular groat seed is roasted, it is called kasha or kashi, which is a Russian staple dish. Toasted groats have a nutty flavor.

millet

A highly digestible, small, white grain that is nonglutenous like quinoa and buckwheat.

quinoa

Known as the Mother Grain from South America, quinoa is a staple in my kitchen. Is it in yours? Maybe not yet, but it will be soon. My personal favorite brand is Ancient Harvest, which makes organic flakes, flour, and grains. The grains come in a colorful selection of red or white. The red has a nutty taste and can be mixed with the white to make an eye-popping and appealing dish.

Replace pasta and bread with quinoa and you will lose weight. Another amazing benefit to using quinoa instead of wheat is a reduction of inflammation throughout the body, thereby reducing pain. Because it is gluten-free, digestion of this wonder grain is easy. It is also not addictive like wheat can be. High in protein, quinoa, like buckwheat, contains eight essential amino acids.

This is great news for anyone who would like to help their digestion by eliminating animal protein at their evening meal and replacing it with quinoa, vegetables, and toasted sesame oil, for example. Combine this versatile grain with spices like turmeric and cumin for more increased digestion, absorption, and—yes, elimination. Quinoa is truly a wonder food for beauty and weight loss!

Quinoa can be boiled, baked, braised, or fried. Its texture can be soft-heavy-moist or fluffy-light-dry. If you are new to this grain, start off with half basmati rice and half quinoa. Grains cook in 15 minutes. Use water, organic veggie broth, spices, fruit juices, or almond milk to make savory and sweet dishes using quinoa. Deepen color with beet or carrot juice for the creative cook in you.

WWW.QUINOA.NET

quinoa flakes

Partially cooked and flaked quinoa. Makes a great breakfast cereal that cooks up in 90 seconds. Flakes can also be added to muffins and pancakes as a gluten-free alternative to wheat flour. Quinoa flakes and grains are used every day in my pantry.

setting up your dairy-free pantry

I like using dairy-free products as much as possible for better digestion. Most of the recipes in this cookbook use dairy-free ingredients, but not all do, and you are always free to substitute. For example, you may replace butter with vegetable butter, and shortening with vegetable shortening. Yogurt may be switched out for unflavored soy yogurt, unsweetened soy milk, or unsweetened almond milk.

Setting up your dairy-free pantry is easy. If you are worried about small amounts of gluten hidden in the malted barley used to make rice syrup, which is the main sweetener used to sweeten most sweetened alternative milks, like almond milk, rice milk, hemp milk, soy milk, hazelnut milk, and oat milk, I suggest using unsweetened almond milk and unsweetened soy milk which can be found in 32-ounce containers. To sweeten, just add 1 tablespoon of agave and 2 droppers of Liquid Stevia Vanilla Crème for a sweet, gluten-free milk alternative.

∽⚬⌒ DAIRY-FREE MILKS

To make your own gluten-free, sweetened nut milk, place 2 cups raw, unsalted organic cashews in a high-powered blender and cover with water to the top of the nuts. Add 1 cup ice and purée. Add 2 tablespoons light agave and 2 droppers of Liquid Stevia Vanilla Crème and blend until smooth. The same recipe can be duplicated with hempseeds. For both cashews and hemp, no overnight soaking is needed.

To make almond milk, soak 2 cups of raw, unsalted organic almonds in 3 cups of water overnight. Drain and rinse nuts then add to high-powered blender. Cover almonds with water to the top of the nuts. Add 1 cup of ice and purée. Add 2 tablespoons light agave and 2 droppers Liquid Stevia Vanilla Crème and blend until smooth. Keeps for several days in the refrigerator.

almond milk

If almond milk is store bought, it's usually made from almonds and sweetened with brown rice syrup that contains malted barley, which is glutenous. Almond milk also comes unsweetened and is made by Blue Diamond, or it's easy to make your own gluten-free, low-glycemic almond milk, cashew milk (see above).

hemp milk

Made from organic hempseeds and contains 7 grams of fat and over a gram of omega-3 per 8-ounce serving. Hemp milk is also available unsweetened, and it's easy to make your own gluten-free, low-glycemic milk from hempseeds (see page 40).

WWW.MANITOBAHARVEST.COM

rice milk

Made from rice and sweetened with brown rice syrup or corn syrup.

soy milk

Made from soybeans and sweetened with brown rice syrup or corn syrup. Unsweetened soy milk is also available. It usually has 9 grams of fat per serving, but because it is not sweetened, I really like the effect on my body—I tend to drink a lot less of it compared to a sweetened milk alternative.

DAIRY-FREE SUBSTITUTES

A few recipes in this cookbook are made with real dairy, like heavy cream and agave for a whipped dessert topping, but you may use a cashew cream in its place. Remember, there are always substitutes. In the following section, I give you healthy alternatives to the dairy I use in the recipes or dairy-free substitutes primarily using unsweetened soy so as to avoid the hidden gluten in malted corn and barley used to sweeten products like almond milk and rice milk.

Although I avoid the gluten found in grains like wheat and barley at all costs, when I don't have time to make my own dairy-free milk or don't have an unsweetened almond milk on hand, I sometimes use almond milk and rice milk which contain small amounts of gluten found in brown rice syrup. If you want to be absolutely gluten-free, make your own nut or seed milk (see page 40).

butter

May be substituted with coconut butter or cream. Used in desserts, coconut butter is the coconut flesh or meat blended with coconut oil. It is a whole food and can be blended in smoothies or melted and used as a base in raw chocolates.

buttermilk, low-fat

May be substituted with 1 cup unsweetened soy milk and ½ teaspoon lemon juice for each cup of low-fat buttermilk.

cow's milk or powdered nonfat milk

May be substituted with any milk alternative like almond or unsweetened soy. For powdered nonfat dry milk (like in the recipe for my Toddler Teething Biscuits), substitute ½ cup nonfat dry milk with ¼ cup pure rice protein powder and ¼ cup milk alternative.

heavy cream

Used for whipped topping on desserts and sweetened with light agave. To make a dairy-free whipped cream, take 1 cup raw, unsalted macadamia nuts, 1 cup raw, unsalted cashews, ½ cup unsweetened almond milk, 2 tablespoons light agave, 2 droppers Liquid Stevia Vanilla Crème, and place in high-powered blender. Blend until smooth. Serve immediately.

shortening and vegetable shortening sticks

Can come in all-natural vegetable-oil-blend sticks that need refrigeration or can come in containers that are shelf stable. All natural shortening is vegan and can be made from a combination of these oils: palm oil, canola oil, soybean oil, olive oil, or sunflower oil. Also available are shortening sticks made with half butter/half vegetable oil that can be found in the refrigerated dairy section of the store.

sour cream

May be substituted with Greek-style yogurt for a healthy dairy substitute, unflavored soy yogurt for a dairy-free substitute, or unsweetened soy milk.

yogurt

May be substituted with unflavored soy yogurt or unsweetened soy milk.

vegetable butter

Can come in a tub as a buttery spread made from a vegetable-oil blend of palm oil, canola oil, soybean oil, olive oil, and/or sunflower oil.

other staples

❧ GOOD OILS

monounsaturated fats

These oils can be used for cooking and baking: almond oil, grapeseed oil, and peanut oil. Extra-virgin olive oil and avocado are monounsaturated fats that are best used cold on salads.

polyunsaturated fats

These oils should be cold-pressed only and not used for cooking since heat damages these fats: flaxseed oil, chia seed oil, hempseed oil, sunflower oil, safflower oil, and sesame oil.

WWW.MANITOBAHARVEST.COM

saturated fats

Butter, extra-virgin coconut oil, and palm oil are the most desirable fats for cooking and baking.

WWW.NUTIVA.COM

WWW.GARDENOFLIFE.COM

WWW.NATURESBLESSINGS.COM

❧ NUT AND SEED BUTTERS

Organic, raw, unsalted tahini, hemp butter, almond butter, cashew butter, black tahini, peanut butter, macadamia nut butter, and sunflower butter.

WWW.MANITOBAHARVEST.COM

let's make a list and get shopping

Making a shopping list is easy and is my key to success. I only use three sugar alternatives, agave, stevia, and zeratol, while gluten-free flour and xanthan gum take care of most recipes calling for wheat flour. Everything else is a whole food and can be found at your local market.

Most of the ingredients you already have in your pantry. The best thing you can do is to make a top-15 list of the new and exciting items. They may sound exotic, but soon will become second-nature staples in your pantry. Start with one recipe. Write down all the ingredients you don't have or have no idea where to find. If you live near a health food store, make a field trip, and if they don't carry your items, ask them to special order or you can purchase ingredients online.

The top-15 sugar-free, gluten-free pantry items below are my "can't live without" foods and just suggestions to get started. These items, along with your regular pantry ingredients, make my famous 90-second gourmet truffle called Fudge It, as well as Pumpkin Pancakes, No Guilt Brownies, plus lots more. You can also pick your own recipe and make a top-15 list to suit you!

∾ KELLY'S TOP 15

The best rule of thumb is if you crave it, make it. But make sure it's sugar-free, gluten-free, and guilt-free. It's important to listen to your body, mind, and spirit. Give yourself what you need in the form of a satisfying and healthy treat. Start with these top-15 ingredients to build your pantry and recipe repertoire. All of the alternative ingredients and superfoods found in this chapter are available at www.kellykeough.com

AGAVE NECTAR

ALL-PURPOSE GLUTEN-FREE FLOUR

BUCKWHEAT GROATS

CACAO, RAW, NIBS

CACAO, RAW, POWDER

CAROB POWDER, ROASTED

COCONUT OIL

ERYTHRITOL/OLIGOFRUCTOSE

GOJI BERRIES

HEMPSEED

HEMP BUTTER

LIQUID STEVIA, CHOCOLATE

LIQUID STEVIA, VANILLA CRÈME

QUINOA

XANTHAN GUM

techniques and tips

∾ SUGAR-FREE BAKING TECHNIQUES AND TIPS

Pick a recipe with a best friend or baking buddy, pitch in for ingredients, and divide them in half to get an inexpensive jump-start to your sugar-free pantry. Most recipes use agave and stevia, which are affordable, inexpensive, and good investments in your health.

Replacing sugar in a recipe is about wanting to eat sweets without having to endure the ill side effects of processed white sugar. My intention is to not only make a dessert or dish that is sugar-free, but one that also cuts out unnecessary carbs and calories. Agave and yacon have low GI's and stevia and zeratol have zero GI's and no calories.

Sugar liquifies in the baking or heating process, so agave is one of the best replacements for sugar in baking and cooking. Like sugar, agave gives volume, moistness, sweetness, browning, and caramelization to the recipe. Agave is also a great choice because the taste is so delicious. Use ⅔ or ¾ cup of agave, depending on the recipe's requirement for moisture and sweetness, for 1 cup of white sugar.

Use a combination of sugar-free alternatives because the blending of the flavors creates the sweetest taste that will satisfy people who still have the taste buds for white sugar and white flour (especially kids who are exposed to that food in their daily life outside the home).

Recipes that call for 1½ cups of sugar can be replaced with ½ cup of agave (light or dark), 2 to 3 droppers of a liquid stevia, and ½ cup of Swerve or ZSweet or an erythritol product. Using this combination will extend the value of your sugar-free pantry, especially because erythritol has a high price point. Replacement volume does not match, but the other liquids or fruit in the recipe will make up for the missing white sugar volume. Also, if you want a sweeter-tasting product, increase agave by 2 tablespoons in a given recipe. For a taste most like sugar, Swerve is the best erythritol choice.

Eating is also a technique. A sugar-free, gluten-free dessert recipe is still a dessert. If you are making cookies, have two. If it is anything else, all you need is one. All recipes in this cookbook should be portioned controlled.

GLUTEN-FREE BAKING TECHNIQUES AND TIPS

Wheat, rye, barley, spelt, and oats (because of cross-contamination with wheat fields), are the popular grains that have gluten, a gluey protein chain that gives baked goods their form, rise, and hold-it-togetherness. Baking wheat-free and gluten-free means there are none of these sticky helper properties. To replace the gluten, use about 1 teaspoon of xanthan gum with a combination of gluten-free flours. My favorite gluten-free flour is an all-purpose flour that already combines garbanzo, fava, tapioca, and potato starch for you. This flour is great for cookies, muffins, and scones.

Silicone bakeware is best for sticky gluten-free dough and batters because it doesn't have to be oiled and dusted. If you are using silicone baby Bundt trays, you may want to spray-oil them, but no dusting is needed.

Dough and batter are best dealt with a long, flat spatula that has been spray-oiled.

Glass baking dishes are good for brownies if you don't have silicone, but any bakeware will do if you properly prepare it with a light coat of spray oil and a dusting of gluten-free flour.

Spray-oil your hands for touching sticky gluten-free dough and batter. You may also spray oil the back of a flat dry measuring cup to even out tart dough or to flatten rounded cookies.

White rice flour is the absolute best for dusting spray-oiled bakeware and for rolling out dough between two sheets of wax paper. Its grainy, nonstick texture acts as an excellent barrier between the dough or batter and your hands or bakeware.

Foil tents used over pies, coffee cakes, breads, and scones—basically all baked goods—will save your masterpieces and ensure they will turn golden and not burn. To make a foil tent, fold a large piece of aluminum foil into quarters and cut a semicircle four inches from the end of folded corner. Open up the foil to reveal a large circle and tent it over prepared batter in prepared baking dish or tin.

Oven thermometers are key in monitoring your baking or roasting temperatures. Gluten-free flours tend to brown quickly and an overheated oven will burn your dough, batter, or crust.

Note that if you don't have a dehydrator, you can still make my dehydrator cookies. Place cookies on a parchment-lined baking sheet and bake at 200 degrees for one hour, then turn the cookies over and bake for an additional 30 minutes.

✥ KITCHEN EQUIPMENT AND BAKEWARE

HIGH-POWERED BLENDER (VITA-MIX)

11-CUP FOOD PROCESSOR

3-CUP MINI-FOOD PROCESSOR

5-TRAY EXCALIBUR DEHYDRATOR WITH TEFLEX SHEETS AND MESH SHEETS

STAND-UP MIXER WITH WIRE WHISK AND PADDLE ATTACHMENTS

SMALL, MEDIUM, AND LARGE MIXING BOWLS

MEDIUM SAUCEPAN, LARGE SKILLET, AND 8-QUART SOUP POT

9-INCH GLASS PIE PLATE

8x8x2-INCH GLASS BAKING DISH AND CAKE PAN

9x12x2-INCH GLASS BAKING DISH

BAKING SHEETS

ROASTING PAN

ROLLING PIN WITH SLEEVE AND PASTRY CLOTH OR MAT

LIQUID AND DRY MEASURING CUPS

MEASURING SPOONS

1-OUNCE SHOT GLASS

STURDY SIFTER

LONG AND SHORT SILICONE SPATULAS

NONSTICK FRYING PAN

WAFFLE IRON

PANCAKE GRIDDLE

SMALL WIRE STRAINER

LARGE COLANDER

LARGE WIRE STRAINER

VEGETABLE PEELER

HEAVY-DUTY COFFEE GRINDER

ICE CREAM MAKER

LARGE METAL AND SILICONE CUPCAKE MOLDS

MINI METAL AND SILICONE CUPCAKE MOLDS

TWO 9x1-INCH CAKE TINS

12-CUP SILICONE BUNDT CAKE PAN

CUTTING BOARDS

FRUIT AND VEGETABLE JUICER

IF YOU CRAVE THAT	EAT THIS
FUDGE	FUDGE IT
CAKE	MIAMI BEACH BIKINI CAKE
BRAN MUFFINS	COURAGEOUS CARROT CAKE MUFFINS
FROZEN YOGURT	ICE CREAM ANY DAY
JELLY OR JAM	STRAWBERRY SLAM JAM
PEANUT BUTTER COOKIES	PEANUT BUTTER BARS
SUGAR, HONEY, MAPLE SYRUP, RICE SYRUP	STEVIA, AGAVE, SWERVE, ZSWEET
MACAROONS	SMACKY MACKYS
APPLE PIE	FOUR APPLE DESSERT
BAGEL	WHOLLY CINNAMON RAISIN BAGEL
SCONES	CAROB CHIP SCONES
CEREAL	KOO KOO COCOA CEREAL
BREAD	THE OTHER WHITE LOAF
OATMEAL COOKIES	OATMEAL WHEELS DEHYDRATOR COOKIES
CHOCOLATE PUDDING	LOVE DOVE CAROB PUDDING
CHOCOLATE MOUSSE	BABY MOUSSE MUD
CHOCOLATE CHIP COOKIES	CLEAVAGE CHIP COOKIES ON A STICK
PUMPKIN PIE	KELLY'S PUMPKIN PIE
SWEET MUFFINS	MAGIC MUFFINS WITH GREAT GANACHE
FUDGE BROWNIES	NO GUILT BROWNIES
ALMOND JOY	ALMOND JOY CUPS
SUGAR COOKIES	CUTOUT SUGAR COOKIES
WAFFLES	WICKED AWESOME PEANUT BUTTER WAFFLES

fudge it: let's get baking

No Guilt Brownies is the very first recipe that kicked off my career and a sugar-free, gluten-free food practice, but it was the Fudge It recipe that saved my life. It also tastes amazingly like chocolate fudge without all the real physical side effects you can get from eating condensed white sugar. This fake fudge recipe is the foundation for all that I am: self-starting, self-confident, and self-healing.

I remember committing wholeheartedly to myself on December 14, 2004 that not one more grain of sugar would pass my lips. Why did it have to be Christmas time? I wondered for only about a day. That was how desperate I was to heal myself. I got through the holidays, even New Year's miraculously. I was on a pink cloud. Yet six weeks into it, I was unraveling and I started craving sugar just like anyone in a diet mentality who happens to be a sugar addict and compulsive overeater. I racked my brain for what to do about the fact I was never going to eat sugar again.

How could I cheat the system? And save time doing it? Now here was a problem that if I solved it would give me self-confidence, and it did. My creativity took over as I studied all the different raw, vegan desserts at my local health food store called Erewhon Market in Hollywood. It was there that I found ingredients that I could eat, sugar- and gluten-free, and that were whole and unrefined. This was the start of my desire to make desserts that not only I could eat, but were healing combinations for my body, mind, and spirit. Not only did I satisfy my sweet tooth without sugar, I taught myself how to not compulsively overeat as well.

⤙❦⤚ FUDGE IT

Fudge It is one of my signature recipes because it is the easiest to make, costs the least because of a small amount of ingredients, and symbolizes the core foundation of my food philosophy: Making desserts and sweets with all-natural ingredients is possible and desirable.

This is the supreme recipe, the absolute winner of the Trophy of Excellence. I ordain us all, once and forevermore, as the secret keepers of the truth that life is not a box of chocolates, but instead, a ball of fudge. Carob fudge, that is. The benefits of this are two fold. One, carob has no caffeine, is a light sweetener, has no fat, and costs under five dollars. The second benefit is that all of my recipes that use cocoa or raw cacao also use carob, and so this recipe is a great way to start building your new pantry. You'll also gather the following ingredients: agave, stevia, vanilla, cinnamon, and some kind of dairy-free milk. Agave is a plant-based, low-glycemic syrup that tastes like honey. Stevia is a green-leafed herb from South America that has no calories and when used with agave has a supersweet taste with no bitter aftertaste. Vanilla and cinnamon are in everyone's pantry, and cinnamon is a circulatory- and metabolism-boosting spice that is a great energy elixir for women when it's combined with carob. The health and beauty benefits also include raw tahini, a sesame butter high in polyunsaturated fats and a great source of iron. You may also roll this fudge into a ball and cover in unsweetened coconut. Very pleasing to the eye, just two of these balls will satisfy your sweet tooth!

How sweet it is to have your fudge and eat it, too! Remember, the key to success is to keep your blood sugar as even as possible, even when eating snacks. At least once month, we all have cravings for chocolate and something decadent (especially if sex is not an option at the moment). So, I propose that we use this confection the instant we get the notion that we need a kiss!

◦◦◦ THE FINAL NOTE ABOUT THIS RECIPE:

This is also the basic foundation recipe for my famous Hemp Ball Truffles that I have been making in my Whole Foods Market Chef Demos in Southern California and New York City.

last looks…

In planning, preparing, and enjoying these recipes, you'll find an abundance of sweetness. And isn't that what life is all about? Sweet pleasure? The reason that you'll be able to have your sweets and eat them, too, without feeling a compulsion to overeat, is because there is no refined white sugar or wheat flour to trigger a biochemical reaction of addiction in your brain chemistry, nor will eating the recipes that follow elicit feelings of guilt and other negative connotations most women associate with carbs and dessert thanks to the diet crazes of popular culture.

Practicing sugar-free and gluten-free is easy with the Three "P's" and the Top 15 Ingredients. At least once a week, make at least three sweets: a dessert, a snack, and a breakfast item.

This food practice is aimed at putting the sweet back into life and, therefore, the pleasure. When is the last time you had a pleasurable meal?

Again and again, here's to your culinary destiny…

brownies and cookies

No Guilt Brownies, Oatmeal Wheels Dehydrator Cookies, and Cry Babies are some of the first snacks I made to satisfy my sweet tooth when I committed to living sugar-free and gluten-free back on December 14, 2004. That was a cold day. I thought my life was over. Yet, in California the chilly weather doesn't last for long, and I soon had the suspicion that a new life was about to begin.

I start with brownies and cookies, the very snacks everyone relates to and craves at least at some point during the day. No Guilt Brownies are made with surprising ingredients: black beans, dates, and tahini. Not only are these brownies satisfying, they can pose as a breakfast staple or an afternoon snack. Oatmeal Wheels Dehydrator Cookies use gluten-free oats grown from designated oat fields, yet some people with celiac disease still may not tolerate oats period, even if the label reads "gluten-free." (If you don't have a dehydrator yet, try Oatmeal Raisin Cookies.) And Cry Babies are a soft, cakey cookie that my great-grandmother used to make for my mother when she was a child. I love the name of the cookie so much, I made it on my cooking show, *The Sweet Truth*, on Veria TV.

Brownies are especially an indulgence for women, and I find that women are most likely to try brownies as their first go-to recipe baked with alternative ingredients. No Guilt Brownies is the official first recipe in my collection. I did so much research on its ingredients, and careful thought went into the taste factor as well as the healing benefits of the recipe. It uses a small amount of buckwheat flour, but you can use any of the alternative flours: all-purpose gluten-free flour with a mix of bean flours, brown rice flour, and even quinoa flour.

Other brownie recipes include Hemp Brownies and Carrot Cake Brownies. I use roasted carob because it is sweeter and doesn't clump like raw carob. When I use cocoa, I use Valrhona powdered cocoa and Scharffen Berger unsweetened 99 percent cocoa baking bars. I also incorporate raw cacao powder and nibs, which are unroasted and full of antioxidants and polyphenols. You'll find these two ingredients in Sicily Biscotti and Allergy-Free Chocolate Chip Cookies.

I've included several traditional chocolate chip cookie recipes that use grain-sweetened chocolate chips, but these chips are not gluten-free, so I have given you options for gluten-free chocolate chips, as well as substitutions for milk and butter using dairy-free alternatives. Brownies and cookies go great with cold unsweetened almond milk, soy milk, and hemp milk with a touch of agave for added sweetness.

NO GUILT BROWNIES

HEMP BROWNIES

FUDGEY BROWNIES

CARROT CAKE BROWNIES

EASY ALMOND CAROB CLUSTERS

FRUIT AND NUT COOKIES

ALLERGY-FREE CHOCOLATE CHIP COOKIES

OATMEAL RAISIN COOKIES

YAM GINGERBREAD PEOPLE

OLD-FASHIONED RASPBERRY THUMBPRINTS

MEXICAN WEDDING CAKES

CAROB PROTEIN DEHYDRATOR COOKIES

OATMEAL WHEELS DEHYDRATOR COOKIES

CHOCOLATE CHIP COOKIES

PEANUT BUTTER PAWS

CLEAVAGE CHIP COOKIES ON A STICK

CRY BABIES

COCONUT SMACKY MACKYS

GODDESS GUCCIDOTTI

CUTOUT SUGAR COOKIES

SICILY BISCOTTI

no guilt brownies

A protein-packed brownie that serves as a meal, snack, or dessert.

2 omega-3 eggs

¼ cup plus 2 tablespoons agave

1½ tablespoons vanilla

¾ cup coconut-date rolls, or chopped Medjool dates

½ cup unsweetened almond milk

1 can (15 ounces) organic black beans, drained

½ cup organic raw tahini, unsalted

3 droppers Liquid Stevia Chocolate

2 teaspoons cinnamon

¾ cup roasted carob powder

½ cup all-purpose gluten-free flour

1 teaspoon gluten-free baking powder

1 teaspoon baking soda

1 teaspoon xanthan gum

¾ cup unsweetened carob chips

½ cup chopped Brazil nuts

Preheat oven to 350 degrees. Spray-oil an 8x8-inch glass baking dish or pan and lightly dust with buckwheat flour; set aside.

Add eggs, agave, and vanilla to food processor. Purée until mixed. Add dates and almond milk and purée until well blended. Add black beans, tahini, stevia, and cinnamon. Pulse until well blended. Add carob powder and pulse slowly until the batter is mixed and looks like the consistency of a brownie mix.

In separate small bowl, blend flour, baking powder, baking soda, and xanthan gum. Slowly add dry mixture to wet mixture in food processor. Pulse until just blended. The brownie mixture will appear very thick. Add in carob chips and pulse a few times.

Transfer the mixture to prepared baking dish. Use a bit of spray oil on your spatula for easy spreading of the batter. Spread brownie mixture evenly and sprinkle chopped Brazil nuts on top. Bake for 45–50 minutes. Brownies are done when a toothpick inserted into the center comes out clean. Cool on a wire rack.

Yield: **16 BROWNIES**

hemp brownies

A rich brownie with the many benefits of hemp's omega-3, -6, and -9 oils.

2 omega-3 eggs

½ cup plus 2 tablespoons agave

2 tablespoons extra-virgin
coconut oil, melted

1½ tablespoons organic vanilla

½ cup coconut-date rolls,
or chopped Medjool dates

½ cup unsweetened almond milk

1 can (15 ounces) navy beans

½ cup hemp butter

3 droppers Liquid Stevia
Vanilla Crème

2 droppers Liquid Stevia
Chocolate

2 teaspoons cinnamon

½ cup carob powder

¼ cup raw cacao powder

3 tablespoons maca powder

½ cup brown rice flour

1 teaspoon gluten-free
baking powder

1 teaspoon xanthan gum

½ cup hempseeds, plus
extra for topping

Preheat oven to 350 degrees. Spray-oil an 8x8-inch glass baking dish or pan and lightly dust with brown rice flour; set aside.

In stand-up mixer with paddle attachment, beat eggs, agave, melted coconut oil, and vanilla. In a food processor, purée dates and almond milk, then add beans, hemp butter, liquid stevias, and cinnamon. Purée again until well mixed. Add this batter to egg mixture in stand-up mixer and blend until well mixed.

Slowly add in carob powder, cacao, and maca and blend until the mixture looks like a brownie batter. In a separate bowl, blend flour, baking powder, and xanthan gum. Slowly add prepared dry mixture to wet mixture and blend. The brownie mixture will feel thick. Fold in ½ cup hempseeds.

Spray-oil a spatula for easy spreading and spoon batter into prepared baking dish. Sprinkle extra hempseeds on top and then drizzle the remaining 2 tablespoons agave over seeds in a crisscross pattern. Bake for 45 minutes or until a toothpick inserted into the middle comes out clean. Cool on a wire rack.

Yield: **16 BROWNIES**

fudgey brownies

A good old-fashioned brownie with no sugar or gluten.

½ cup butter or vegetable butter

4 ounces unsweetened baking chocolate

½ cup agave

¾ cup Swerve

1½ tablespoons vanilla extract

2 droppers Liquid Stevia Vanilla Crème

2 droppers Liquid Stevia Chocolate

3 omega-3 eggs

½ cup all-purpose gluten-free flour

½ teaspoon gluten-free baking powder

½ teaspoon xanthan gum

Preheat oven to 350 degrees. Spray-oil an 8x8-inch glass baking dish or pan and dust with unsweetened cocoa powder; set aside.

Place butter and chocolate in double boiler on medium heat and melt, stirring constantly, 6–7 minutes. Remove from heat. Stir in agave, Swerve, vanilla, and liquid stevias. Whisk in eggs one at a time. In small mixing bowl, combine flour, baking powder, and xanthan gum. Gently fold dry mixture into wet chocolate mixture.

Pour batter into prepared pan. Use a spray-oiled spatula to scrape down sides of bowl. Bake 40–45 minutes. Brownies are done when a toothpick inserted into the center comes out clean. Cool on wire rack.

Yield: 16 BROWNIES

carrot cake brownies

A healthy twist on a blondie.

1½ cups all-purpose gluten-free flour

1 teaspoon gluten-free baking powder

½ teaspoon baking soda

1 teaspoon xanthan gum

2 teaspoons cinnamon

½ cup agave

½ cup yacon syrup or coconut sugar

½ cup Swerve

2 omega-3 eggs

½ cup extra-virgin coconut oil, melted

1 tablespoon vanilla extract

1½ cups shredded carrot

½ cup unsweetened coconut

¾ cup chopped walnuts

Preheat oven to 350 degrees. Spray-oil an 8x8-inch glass baking dish or pan and dust with gluten-free flour; set aside.

In stand-up mixer, blend gluten-free flour, baking powder, baking soda, xanthan gum, and cinnamon. Add agave, yacon syrup, Swerve, eggs, melted oil, and vanilla and mix until thoroughly combined. Add carrots, coconut, and walnuts and blend until just combined.

Spray-oil a spatula and spread batter into the prepared baking dish. Bake for 25–30 minutes. Brownies are done when a toothpick inserted into the center comes out clean. Cool on a wire rack.

Yield: **16 BROWNIES**

easy almond carob clusters

A recipe with few ingredients to get you started baking cookies.

1½ cups whole raw almonds

¼ cup extra-virgin coconut oil, melted

½ cup agave

1 large omega-3 egg

1 tablespoon vanilla extract

½ cup roasted carob

½ cup all-purpose gluten-free flour

Preheat oven to 300 degrees. Spread almonds on a cookie sheet and toast in oven for 20 minutes to bring out oils and enhance flavor. Remove almonds from oven; set aside to cool. Increase oven temperature to 350 degrees. Line cookie sheet with parchment paper; set aside.

In food processor, blend coconut oil and agave until smooth, about 3 minutes. Add egg, vanilla, and carob and pulse to mix. Add flour and pulse to mix. Scrape batter out of food processor and into bowl; stir in almonds.

Drop cookie dough by rounded teaspoons onto prepared baking sheet. Bake for 10–12 minutes. Cool cookies on wire rack.

Yield: 24 COOKIES

fruit and nut cookies

A fruit and nut cookie sweetened with dates and agave. The original recipe calls for whole-wheat flour and is from my friend Koji.

½ cup vegetable butter or butter, softened

1 omega-3 egg

2 teaspoons vanilla

¼ cup agave

1 cup all-purpose gluten-free flour

1 teaspoon gluten-free baking powder

⅛ teaspoon salt

1 cup unsweetened coconut

1 cup coconut-date rolls, or Medjool dates

2 teaspoons orange zest

1 cup pecans, finely chopped

In food processor, blend the butter, egg, and vanilla. Add agave and blend until smooth. In small mixing bowl, combine the flour, baking powder, and salt. Add the dry mixture a little at a time to the creamed mixture in the food processor and pulse until just combined.

Cut coconut-date rolls into small pieces. In medium bowl, combine coconut-date roll pieces, orange zest, and ½ cup of the pecans. Add to food processor and pulse 3–4 times until date mixture is just combined into the cookie mixture.

Scrape out cookie dough from food processor and place on a work surface covered with wax paper and lightly floured with gluten-free flour. Divide the dough in half and form into two logs, approximately 1½ inches in diameter.

Place the remaining ½ cup of pecans on wax paper. Roll the logs in the nuts. Wrap each log in wax paper and chill for 1 hour.

Preheat oven to 350 degrees. To bake, slice the logs into ⅛-inch rounds and place them on an ungreased cookie sheet. Bake for 10–12 minutes until lightly browned. Cool on a wire rack.

Yield: **24 COOKIES**

allergy-free chocolate chip cookies

A chocolate chip cookie with no flour, butter, sugar, or eggs.

1½ cup sprouted buckwheat groats
(See note on sprouting)

¼ cup soaked golden flaxseeds
(See note on soaking)

1 apple with skin, chopped

¼ cup light agave

3 droppers Liquid Stevia
Vanilla Crème

1 dropper Liquid Stevia
Chocolate

3 tablespoons Swerve

2 teaspoons vanilla extract

⅓ cup raw cacao nibs

Place sprouted buckwheat and soaked flaxseeds in food processor with S-blade attachment. Add chopped apple, agave, liquid stevias, Swerve, and vanilla. Purée about one minute until all ingredients are well blended.

With a spatula, scrape batter into a medium mixing bowl. Stir in cacao nibs.

Using two spoons, spoon-drop 1 tablespoon of the batter for each cookie onto a Teflex sheet. Place four across and four down for 16 cookies a sheet.

Dehydrate at 105 degrees for 18 hours. Halfway through, you may use a thin metal spatula to lift cookie off Teflex sheet, place on mesh sheet, and continue to dehydrate for a crisper cookie.

Yield: **48 COOKIES**

Sprouting Note: Start soaking and sprouting the buckwheat groats several days before. In a covered container, soak 1 cup raw buckwheat groats in 2 cups filtered water overnight in the refrigerator. In the morning, drain groats into a large colander and spread the groats evenly around the sides with a flat spatula. Place a plate underneath the colander to catch dripping water. Cover the colander with a paper towel and let the groats sprout on the counter, out of the sun in a cool, dry place, for 36–48 hours. When you see a little white tail pop out of the groats, sprouting is complete. Place sprouted groats in a container and refrigerate until ready to use. Measure 1½ cups of sprouted buckwheat groats for recipe.

Soaking Note: Soak ⅔ cup golden flaxseeds with 1½ cups water overnight in refrigerator. Flaxseeds may stay soaked in water for up to one week until ready to use. Drain any leftover liquid before use.

oatmeal raisin cookies

A chewy oatmeal cookie using gluten-free oats and yacon syrup.

1 cup raisins

½ cup spiced apple cider

1 teaspoon cinnamon

¾ cup butter or vegetable butter

¾ cup Swerve

½ cup agave

½ cup yacon syrup
or coconut sugar

1 omega-3 egg

1 tablespoon vanilla extract

1½ cups all-purpose
gluten-free flour

1 teaspoon gluten-free
baking powder

½ teaspoon baking soda

1 teaspoon xanthan gum

1 cup unsweetened coconut

2 cups gluten-free
old-fashioned rolled oats

Start the day before by soaking raisins, apple cider, and cinnamon in a small bowl covered with a lid overnight in the refrigerator.

Preheat oven to 350 degrees. Line baking sheets with parchment paper; set aside.

In stand-up mixer with paddle attachment, cream butter and Swerve until fluffy, about 3 minutes. Add in agave and yacon syrup and mix until smooth. Add in egg and vanilla and mix well, scraping down sides when needed.

In medium mixing bowl, sift together gluten-free flour, baking powder, baking soda, and xanthan gum. Add dry mixture to wet mixture and mix until just combined. Fold in coconut and then raisins until just combined.

Using two spoons, spoon-drop large tablespoons of cookie dough onto prepared baking sheets 2 inches apart. Bake for 15 minutes. Cool on baking sheets for 2 minutes and then transfer cookies to cool on wire rack.

Yield: **48 COOKIES**

yam gingerbread people

Yam gives these cookies a holiday pumpkin taste.

1 cup butter or Earth Balance Natural Shortening sticks

½ cup Swerve

½ cup dark agave

⅓ cup yacon syrup or coconut sugar

⅔ cup puréed yam

2 omega-3 eggs

3 droppers Liquid Stevia Cinnamon

3¼ cups all-purpose gluten-free flour

1 teaspoon baking soda

1 teaspoon xanthan gum

1 teaspoon cinnamon

1½ teaspoons ground ginger

½ teaspoon nutmeg

¼ teaspoon ground clove

¼ cup unsweetened almond milk

½ cup raisins, for decorating

In stand-up mixer using paddle attachment, cream shortening and Swerve. Add agave and yacon syrup and mix until smooth. Add yam purée, eggs, and liquid stevia and mix well. In medium mixing bowl, sift flour, baking soda, xanthan gum, cinnamon, ginger, nutmeg, and clove. Slowly add dry mixture into creamed mixture, alternating between flour and almond milk. Dough will be sticky. Form into a ball, place in bowl, and cover with plastic wrap. Chill at least 2 hours.

Preheat oven to 350 degrees. Line baking sheet with parchment paper; set aside.

Prepare work surface by covering a pastry mat with two sheets of wax paper and lightly dust with gluten-free flour. Place a pastry sleeve on rolling pin and generously dust with gluten-free flour. One cookie at a time, scoop out a small handful of the batter and roll into a ball. Roll dough to ¼-inch thick. Decorate cookie with raisins.

Dip cookie cutter into gluten-free flour and cut one cookie at a time. With broad spatula dipped into gluten-free flour, lift cookies off of wax paper and place onto prepared baking sheet. Bake above oven center for about 10–11 minutes or until cookies spring back lightly in center. Do not overbake. Remove from sheets. Cool on wire racks.

Yield: **12 COOKIES**

old-fashioned raspberry thumbprints

Use your favorite all-fruit berry spread in this cookie or make your own raspberry filling.

COOKIES

1 cup butter or Earth Balance 50/50 sticks

1½ cups all-purpose gluten-free flour

½ teaspoon xanthan gum

½ cup Swerve

½ cup agave

3 droppers Liquid Stevia Vanilla Crème

2 omega-3 egg yolks

2 teaspoons vanilla extract

2 omega-3 egg whites, slightly beaten

1 cup walnuts, finely chopped

½ cup raspberry filling (see recipe below) or all-fruit jam

FILLING

2 cups frozen red raspberries

½ cup apple cider

¼ cup Swerve

½ teaspoon finely grated lemon zest

2 teaspoons lemon juice

1 dropper Liquid Stevia Lemon Drops

2 tablespoons agave

2 teaspoons arrowroot

1 tablespoon cold water

For Cookies: In stand-up mixer, cream butter for 2 3 minutes. In small mixing bowl, sift together flour and xanthan gum. Add half of sifted flour mixture to creamed mixture. Add Swerve, agave, liquid stevia, egg yolks, and vanilla. Mix well, scraping down sides when needed. Mix in remaining flour. Cover with plastic wrap and chill for 2 hours.

Preheat oven to 375 degrees. Generously grease cookie sheet with vegetable butter. Shape dough into small, 1-inch balls. Dip balls in egg whites, then roll in walnuts. Place cookies 1 inch apart on the prepared baking sheet. Using your thumb or back of a measuring teaspoon, press an indentation into each cookie. Bake for 5 minutes. With the back of a measuring teaspoon, press the thumbprint back down and continue to bake for another 5–7 minutes. Cool on a wire rack. To serve, fill cooled cookies with a teaspoon of all-fruit spread or make the following raspberry filling.

For Filling: In medium saucepan over medium heat, place raspberries, apple cider, Swerve, lemon zest, lemon juice, liquid stevia, and agave. Stir constantly until raspberries break down and sauce comes to a boil. In small cup, whisk arrowroot with cold water until it is dissolved. Slowly stir arrowroot mixture into raspberries until it is well blended. Cook fruit mixture down until thick, about 10 minutes. Cool raspberry filling before filling cookies.

Yield: **24 COOKIES**

mexican wedding cakes

An all-white cookie with no wheat or sugar for an occasion.

1½ cups confectioners' Swerve

1 cup pecan halves

1½ cups all-purpose gluten-free flour

½ cup tapioca starch

1 teaspoon xanthan gum

¾ cup butter or Earth Balance 50/50 sticks

¼ cup agave

1 tablespoon vanilla extract

½ teaspoon almond extract

Line baking sheet with parchment paper; set aside. In food processor, combine pecans with ¼ cup confectioners' Swerve. Pulse until nuts are finely ground. In large mixing bowl, whisk together the sugar-nut mixture, flour, tapioca starch, and xanthan gum; set aside.

In stand-up mixer with paddle attachment, beat the butter and ¾ cup of confectioners' sugar on high for 3–4 minutes until fluffy. Scrape down sides of bowl when needed. Beat in agave, vanilla, and almond extract. Add dry mixture and mix until dough comes together.

Place remaining confectioners' sugar in a small bowl. Roll dough into small, 1-inch balls and then roll balls in confectioners' sugar. Place 2 inches apart on prepared baking sheets. Freeze prepared cookies for 30 minutes.

Preheat oven to 350 degrees. Bake cookies for 10–12 minutes, rotating racks halfway through the baking process. Cool cookies on a wire rack. Place remaining confectioners' sugar in a small mixing bowl and roll cookies to coat completely. Layer cookies between sheets of wax paper.

Yield: 24 COOKIES

carob protein dehydrator cookies

A high-protein, low-carb cookie made with protein powder, buckwheat groats, and agave.

1 cup sprouted buckwheat groats
(See note on sprouting)

½ cup cooked yam with skin

⅓ cup organic raw tahini, unsalted

3 droppers Liquid Stevia
Vanilla Crème

½ cup rice or lactose-free
whey protein powder

3 tablespoons dark agave

½ cup almond milk

2 teaspoons cinnamon

3 rounded tablespoons
roasted carob

1 rounded tablespoon cocoa powder

1 tablespoon vanilla extract

2 tablespoons ground raw cacao nibs
and goji berries

In food processor, purée all the ingredients until smooth. Spoon 1 rounded tablespoon of the mixture onto Teflex dehydrator sheets with 4 across and 4 down for a total of 16 cookies to a sheet.

With back of spoon in a circular motion, flatten each of the cookies into a ¼-inch-high round shape. Sprinkle each cookie with coconut. Dehydrate at 105 degrees for 16–20 hours depending on how chewy or crunchy you like your cookies. Store in an airtight container for two weeks.

Yield: **36 COOKIES**

Sprouting Note: Start soaking and sprouting the buckwheat groats several days before. In a covered container, soak ¾ cup raw buckwheat groats in 2 cups filtered water overnight in the refrigerator. In the morning, drain groats into a large colander. You may use buckwheat that has been soaked and drained or continue to sprout. To sprout, spread the groats evenly around the sides with a flat spatula. Place a plate underneath the colander to catch dripping water. Cover the colander with a paper towel and let the groats sprout on the counter, out of the sun in a cool, dry place, for 36–48 hours. When you see a little white tail pop out of the groats, sprouting is complete. Place sprouted groats in a container and refrigerate until ready to use. Measure 1 cup of sprouted buckwheat groats for recipe.

oatmeal wheels dehydrator cookies

A chewy, spiced apple cookie with raisins and macadamia nuts.

1½ cup gluten-free old-fashioned rolled oats

¾ cup coconut-date rolls

½ cup spiced apple cider

2 tablespoons dark agave

2 droppers Liquid Stevia Vanilla Crème

2 teaspoons cinnamon

½ cup unsweetened coconut

1 Fuji apple, sliced

¼ cup raisins

¼ cup raw macadamia nuts, coarsely chopped

Gluten-Free Note: Instead of the oats, you may also use 1 cup of soaked buckwheat groats by measuring ¾ cup dry hulled buckwheat groats and soaking in 2 cups water overnight. Eliminate the extra ½ cup of oats at the end of the recipe.

To food processor add the premeasured 1 cup oats, coconut-date rolls, apple cider, agave, liquid stevia, cinnamon, coconut, and sliced apple. Pulse until just combined. Once batter is mixed, purée and blend until batter is smooth.

Scrape out batter from food processor and spoon into medium mixing bowl. Stir in raisins, nuts, and the remaining ½ cup of oats. Measure a rounded tablespoon full for each cookie and form into ½-inch-high flat circles 2 inches in diameter on a Teflex dehydrator baking sheet. Place 16 cookies to a tray. Dehydrate at 105 degrees for 16–20 hours. Halfway through the dehydration process, use a spray-oiled spatula and flip cookies over. Continue to dehydrate. Keep in an airtight container for up to two weeks.

Yield: **24 COOKIES**

chocolate chip cookies

A classic chocolate chip cookie made with your choice of chips.

1 cup vegetable butter or butter or Earth Balance 50/50 sticks

½ cup Swerve

½ cup dark agave

1 omega-3 egg

2 tablespoons vanilla extract

3 droppers Liquid Stevia Vanilla Crème

¼ cup unsweetened coconut

1¾ cups all-purpose gluten-free flour

1 teaspoon gluten-free baking soda

1 teaspoon xanthan gum

¾ cup grain-sweetened chocolate chips (See gluten-free note)

....

Gluten-Free Note: You may use grain-sweetened chocolate chips, but they may contain barley, which contains gluten. Substitute the grain-sweetened chocolate chips with ¾ cup unsweetened carob chips or ½ cup raw cacao nibs for a gluten-free cookie.

Prepare baking sheet with parchment paper; set aside.

In stand-up mixer with paddle attachment, cream butter and Swerve. Mix in agave, egg, vanilla, and liquid stevia. Mix in coconut until just combined.

In small bowl, sift together flour, baking soda, and xanthan gum. Slowly add prepared dry ingredients to wet batter and blend. Stir in grain-sweetened chocolate chips.

Form into 2-inch domes and place on prepared baking sheet. Freeze formed, uncooked cookies for at least 30 minutes. Preheat oven to 350 degrees. Bake for 11–12 minutes. Cool on wire rack.

Yield: **24 SMALL COOKIES**

peanut butter paws

A cookie made with peanut butter and quinoa flour for high protein.

1 cup vegetable butter or butter

½ cup Swerve

1 cup peanut butter

½ cup dark agave

1 omega-3 egg

2 tablespoons vanilla extract

3 droppers Liquid Stevia Vanilla Crème

1 cup quinoa flour

1 cup all-purpose gluten-free flour

1 teaspoon baking soda

1 teaspoon xanthan gum

½ cup raw peanuts, chopped (optional)

Line baking sheet with parchment paper; set aside.

In stand-up mixer with paddle attachment, cream butter and Swerve. Add peanut butter and mix until well blended. Add agave, egg, vanilla, and liquid stevia and mix until well blended.

In small bowl, sift together quinoa flour, gluten-free flour, baking soda, and xanthan gum. Add dry mixture slowly to wet batter and blend. Stir in chopped raw peanuts.

Form into 2-inch domes and place on prepared baking sheet. Spray-oil a fork and make crisscross marks in each cookie. Freeze formed, uncooked cookies for at least 30 minutes. Preheat oven to 350 degrees. Bake for 11–12 minutes. Cool on wire rack.

Yield: **24 SMALL COOKIES**

cleavage chip cookies on a stick

A huge grain-sweetened chocolate chip cookie on a stick.

1 cup pecan halves

2 cups plus 2 tablespoons all-purpose gluten-free flour

2 teaspoons baking soda

2 teaspoons xanthan gum

¾ teaspoon sea salt

1 cup butter or vegetable butter

½ cup Swerve

½ cup dark agave

2 droppers Liquid Stevia Vanilla Crème

2 droppers Liquid Stevia Dark Chocolate

1 omega-3 egg

1 omega-3 egg yolk

2 tablespoons vanilla extract

1½ cups unsweetened puffed brown rice, slightly crushed

¾ cup grain-sweetened chocolate chips (See gluten-free note)

....

Gluten-Free Note: You may use grain-sweetened chocolate chips, but they may contain barley, which contains gluten. Substitute the grain-sweetened chocolate chips with ¾ cup unsweetened carob chips or ½ cup raw cacao nibs for a gluten-free cookie.

Line baking sheets with parchment paper; set aside.

In dry nonstick sauté pan, place pecans over medium heat and toast until oils are released, about 8 minutes. Immediately transfer nuts to a bowl; set aside.

In large mixing bowl, sift together gluten-free flour, baking soda, xanthan gum, and salt; set aside. In medium saucepan, melt butter over medium heat. Turn off the heat under the butter. With wire whisk, add Swerve and agave to butter mixture. Whisk mixture until combined. Pour into large mixing bowl to cool slightly.

Add liquid stevias, egg, egg yolk, and vanilla to melted butter mixture. Add prepared wet mixture to large mixing bowl containing dry mixture and stir until just combined. Gently stir in the crushed puffed rice. Let dough cool completely at room temperature. When cookie dough is cooled, mix in chips and nuts.

With a large spoon, scoop cookie dough onto prepared baking sheets about 2 inches apart. Spray-oil hands so dough will not stick and form dough into balls. Spray-oil the bottom of a small dish and flatten the cookie mounds slightly with the flat bottom and slide off the cookie. Do not pull the small cup directly up or the dough will peal off.

Place a Popsicle or cookie stick in the bottom a third of the way through each cookie at a 45-degree angle and place in the freezer for 30 minutes. Preheat oven to 350 degrees. Bake for 11–13 minutes. Remove from oven and cool for 2 minutes before transferring to wire rack.

Yield: **12 LARGE COOKIES**

cry babies

My great Gran's old-fashioned, soft, cakey cookie with a smiley face.

1 cup butter or vegetable butter

½ cup vanilla rice protein powder

1 omega-3 egg

1 cup unsweetened almond milk

½ cup dark agave

1 tablespoon vanilla extract

2 droppers Liquid Stevia Vanilla Crème

3½ cups all-purpose gluten-free flour

½ cup brown rice flour

3 teaspoons Stevia Plus Powder

2 teaspoons cinnamon

2 teaspoons baking soda

2 teaspoons xanthan gum

½ teaspoon salt

½ cup organic raisins

In stand-up mixer with paddle attachment, cream butter and protein powder. Add in egg, milk, agave, vanilla, and liquid stevia and beat until smooth.

In separate bowl, sift together gluten-free flour, brown rice flour, Stevia Plus Powder, cinnamon, baking soda, xanthan gum, and salt. Slowly add dry ingredients to wet ingredients and blend well. Batter should be soft and fluffy, not dense like a regular cookie dough.

Spoon 12 large spoonfuls onto ungreased cookie sheet spaced evenly. Form into balls and flatten. Decorate face with raisins. Freeze for 30 minutes. Preheat oven to 350 degrees. Bake for 12–15 minutes. Cool on wire rack.

Yield: **36 COOKIES**

coconut smacky mackys

A protein-packed macaroon with vanilla protein powder and agave.

4 large egg whites

¼ teaspoon cream of tartar

1 dropper Liquid Stevia
Vanilla Crème

2 tablespoons light agave

1 teaspoon vanilla extract

½ teaspoon almond extract

2 cups unsweetened
shredded coconut

¼ cup vanilla rice or
lactose-free whey protein powder

2 tablespoons tapioca starch

2 tablespoons almond meal

Preheat oven to 325 degrees. Spray-oil baking sheet and line with parchment paper; set aside.

In stand-up mixer with wire attachment, whisk egg whites and cream of tartar until soft peaks are formed. Add in liquid stevia, agave, vanilla, almond extract, and beat until batter is shiny.

By hand, carefully fold in coconut, protein powder, tapioca starch, and almond meal. Drop mixture by packed tablespoons onto prepared sheet. There should be 16 to a baking sheet. Bake 12–15 minutes. Cookies are done when slightly golden. Be careful not to overbake because cookies will harden. Taste is best when cooled an hour on wire rack.

Yield: **24 COOKIES**

goddess guccidotti

A Christmas fig cookie with sugar-free pink frosting.

DOUGH

1 cup vegetable shortening

1½ cups yacon powder

6 omega-3 eggs

1 tablespoon vanilla extract

pinch salt

3 cups all-purpose gluten-free flour

1 cup potato starch

3 teaspoons gluten-free baking powder

1 teaspoon baking soda

3 teaspoons Stevia Plus Powder

2 teaspoons xanthan gum

FILLING

1 whole orange (with peel), coarsely chopped

1 small Fuji apple (with peel), sliced

1 zest of lemon

1½ cups dried black figs, finely chopped

1 cup raisins

½ cup dark agave

2 droppers Liquid Stevia Valencia Orange

1 cup pecans

2 teaspoons cinnamon

½ teaspoon allspice

For Dough: In stand-up mixer with paddle attachment, cream shortening and yacon powder or Swerve. Add in eggs, vanilla, and salt and beat until smooth. The batter will appear curdled. Make sure to continually scrape down sides of bowl with spatula.

In separate bowl, sift together gluten-free flour, potato starch, baking powder, baking soda, Stevia Plus Powder, and xanthan gum. In stand-up mixer with paddle attachment, slowly blend sifted dry mixture into wet mixture. Knead dough with spray-oiled hands until smooth and workable. Wrap dough in plastic and chill for 2 hours.

For Filling: In food processor, purée chopped orange, sliced apple, and lemon zest. One at a time, slowly add figs, raisins, agave, and liquid stevia by pulse action and then purée. Next pulse in pecans, cinnamon, and allspice and purée. Add extra water to thin if needed. Should make a thick paste.

For Assembly: Preheat oven to 375 degrees. Between two pieces of floured wax paper, roll out ⅓ of the dough into a 5x10-inch rectangle shape about ¼-inch thick. Use a floured knife to shape rectangle and cut off extra dough. Using 4–5 rounded tablespoons, put fig mixture in a line leaving a ½-inch margin from the left side. Fold dough in half lengthwise over fig mixture, sealing sides by pinching dough together with your fingers. This dough is very pliable and can be rolled out many times.

With clean, floured knife, cut cookies about 1½ inches, using a diagonal cut. Wipe the knife clean after every cut. Make small diagonal slits in the sides of the cookies. With spatula, move to a ungreased cookie sheet and bake for 10–12 minutes. Cool on wire rack.

Yield: **36 COOKIES**

FROSTING

1½ cups confectioners' Swerve

2 tablespoons butter or vegetable shortening

2 tablespoons unsweetened almond milk, unsweetened soy milk, or water

1 dropper Liquid Stevia Vanilla Crème

2 teaspoons light agave

1 teaspoon cranberry juice or 2 drops natural food coloring

For Frosting: In stand-up mixer with paddle attachment, cream together confectioners' Swerve and vegetable shortening. Add in milk or water, liquid stevia, agave, and cranberry juice or all-natural food coloring. Repeat recipe if more frosting is needed. Frost cooled cookies.

cutout sugar cookies

A frosted, cakey cutout cookie made with agave—no sugar, wheat, or gluten.

COOKIES

1 cup vegetable shortening

¾ cup Swerve

2 omega-3 eggs

1 tablespoon vanilla extract

1 cup sour cream

½ cup light agave

2 droppers Liquid Stevia
Vanilla Crème

2½ cups all-purpose
gluten-free flour

1 cup white rice flour

1 cup potato starch

2 teaspoons gluten-free
baking powder

1 teaspoon baking soda

1 teaspoon xanthan gum

ICING

1 cup confectioners' Swerve

2 teaspoons unsweetened
almond milk or water

1 dropper Liquid Stevia
Vanilla Crème

2 teaspoons light agave

2 teaspoons cranberry juice
or 2 drops natural food coloring

Note: Use white rice flour for rolling out
dough and for dipping cookie cutters.

For Cookies: In stand-up mixer with paddle attachment, cream shortening and Swerve. Add in eggs and beat until fluffy. Add in vanilla, sour cream, agave, and liquid stevia and blend.

In separate bowl, sift together gluten-free flour, white rice flour, potato starch, baking powder, baking soda, and xanthan gum.

With paddle attachment in stand-up mixer, add sifted dry ingredients to wet ingredients and mix. Scrape down sides of bowl. If needed, add a bit of flour to hands first and then form dough into a ball. Wrap in plastic. Refrigerate 2 hours.

Preheat oven to 350 degrees. Using a pastry sleeve on a rolling pin, roll out dough on lightly dusted wax paper to about ¼ inch thick. Cut out cookies with floured cookie cutters and place on ungreased cookie sheet. This dough is very durable and can be rolled out many times.

Bake for 6 minutes. Watch cookies carefully. Cookies should not brown and should stay white in color. Cookies are done when they spring back to the touch. Cool on wire rack.

For Icing: In stand-up mixer with paddle attachment, combine the confectioners' Swerve, almond milk or water, liquid stevia, agave, and cranberry juice or all-natural coloring and mix well. Beat icing for 2–3 minutes until glossy. Frost cookies with icing when cooled. Repeat icing recipe to frost all five dozen cookies.

Yield: **60 COOKIES**

sicily biscotti

 A fudgey, caffeine-free, mocha-tasting Italian cookie made with roasted maca and agave.

½ cup grain-sweetened
chocolate chips
(See gluten-free note)

2 cups all-purpose
gluten-free flour

1¼ cups brown rice flour

2 teaspoons Stevia Plus Powder

1 teaspoon xanthan gum

½ teaspoon baking soda

½ teaspoon gluten-free
baking powder

⅛ teaspoon sea salt

½ cup butter or vegetable butter,
slightly softened

½ cup Swerve

2 omega-3 eggs

½ cup dark agave

1 tablespoon vanilla extract

½ cup almond meal

2 tablespoons roasted maca
or instant decaf coffee

1½ cups roasted almonds, chopped

Gluten-Free Note: Grain-sweetened chocolate chips may contain malted barley, which contains gluten. For a gluten-free substitute, melt 2 ounces unsweetened baking chocolate in a double-boiler over medium heat. Stir in an extra ¼ cup Swerve or ZSweet and substitute this mixture for melted grain-sweetened chips.

Melt chocolate chips over medium heat in double boiler; set aside.

In medium bowl, sift together gluten-free flour, brown rice flour, Stevia Plus Powder, xanthan gum, baking soda, baking powder, and salt; set aside.

With paddle attachment in stand-up mixer, cream the butter until white. Add the Swerve and beat until fluffy, about 5 minutes. Blend in the eggs, one at a time. Add agave, vanilla, almond meal, maca, and melted chips. Stir in the almonds. With paddle attachment, slowly add the prepared dry ingredients to the wet ingredients to form a firm dough. Wrap dough in plastic and refrigerate dough for 2 hours.

Preheat oven to 375 degrees. Lightly grease two cookie sheets and line with parchment paper; set aside.

Divide the dough into 3 equal pieces. On a floured sheet of wax paper, roll each piece into a log 2 inches thick and 12 inches long. Place 2 logs on one prepared baking sheet, and one log on the second prepared baking sheet, leaving enough space between them for the dough to spread while baking. Bake the logs for 20 minutes.

Let baked logs sit for 10 minutes. With serrated knife, slice the logs about ¾-inch thick on a slight diagonal. Place the slices, cut side down, on the original cookie sheets lined with parchment paper.

Lower the oven temperature to 350 degrees. Bake the slices for 12–15 minutes. Cool on a wire rack. Store in an airtight container.

Yield: **36 COOKIES**

breads, pancakes, cereals, and bars

Sweet breads are the easiest sugar-free, gluten-free recipes to bake because most of them—like Zucchini Bread with Icing, Pumpkin Loaf, and my favorite, Sweet Hot Cherry Corn Bread—can be done by hand in one large mixing bowl.

A sweet corn bread can be made in less than 45 minutes and eaten for breakfast or can accompany a salad for lunch. Made with yogurt, quinoa flour, and quinoa flakes, the corn bread is made with whole, unrefined quinoa flour, which is a good source of protein.

Other sweet breads not only can be eaten for breakfast, they are also satisfying snacks and desserts. For example, Chocolate Gingerbread tastes like chocolate cake. This recipe is one of the sweet breads that uses baked yam, which is puréed in a food processor. Other recipes that use baked yam are Bean Town Brown Bread and Pumpkin Spice Pancakes. While many of the sweet bread recipes can be made in a food processor, like Eve's Apple Cake, the pancake recipes are made in a blender with egg whites. Having a simple process is the key to making these recipes a part of your everyday life. At first, going sugar-free and gluten-free is a surprise and usually the first meal that suffers in taste is breakfast!

Use the recipes in this chapter to make breakfast delicious. Ask yourself, "What do I crave for breakfast?" or "What do my kids always want to eat in the morning?" If you come up with waffles, then there is a Wicked Awesome Peanut Butter Waffle recipe that goes great with banana and agave. Or try a chocolate cereal recipe called Koo Koo Cocoa Cereal. Eaten with unsweetened almond milk or hemp milk, this can be a dairy-free breakfast, too.

The bar recipes also get great meal mileage as on the go pick-me-ups or mini-meals. Any time, anywhere, bars have taken over our world of snacking fashion. Every grocery store, health or conventional, has an entire aisle dedicated to individually wrapped bars to eat in the car. Save money and sugar calories by making your own health bars using the following recipes: Hemp Protein Raw Bars, Raw Cherry Pistachio Seed Bars, and Gluten-Free Blueberry Oat Bars. Note that it is possible that people with celiac disease may not tolerate gluten-free oats. Great alternatives for oats are recipes that use buckwheat, like Blueberry Breakfast Bread.

PUMPKIN LOAF

ZUCCHINI BREAD WITH ICING

BANANA BREAD

CAROB CORN BREAD

IT'S A PIECE OF CORN CAKE

SWEET HOT CHERRY CORN BREAD

CORN BREAD STUFFING

EVE'S APPLE CAKE

BLUEBERRY BREAKFAST BREAD

CHOCOLATE GINGERBREAD

THE OTHER WHITE LOAF

BEAN TOWN BROWN BREAD

CINNAMON TWIST AND SHOUT ROLL-UPS

WICKED AWESOME PEANUT BUTTER WAFFLES

STRAWBERRY SLAM JAM

STAR BUCKWHEAT PANCAKES

PUMPKIN SPICE PANCAKES

VEGAN BLUEBERRY PANCAKES

QUEEN QUINOA

KOO KOO COCOA CEREAL

GREAT LOW-FAT VANILLA GRANOLA

RAW HEMP PROTEIN BARS

GLUTEN-FREE BLUEBERRY OAT BARS

RAW CHERRY PISTACHIO SEED BARS

pumpkin loaf

A moist, pumpkin-spiced sweet bread for breakfast or dessert.

1½ cups all-purpose gluten-free flour

1 teaspoon baking soda

1 teaspoon gluten-free baking powder

1 teaspoon xanthan gum

2 teaspoons pumpkin pie spice

¼ cup ground flaxseeds

½ cup unsweetened almond milk

1 large omega-3 egg

¾ cup Swerve

¼ cup extra-virgin coconut oil, melted

½ cup agave

2 droppers Liquid Stevia Cinnamon

1 can (15 ounces) pumpkin

Preheat oven to 350 degrees. Spray-oil an 8x4x2-inch loaf pan and line with parchment paper; set aside.

Sift together flour, baking soda, baking powder, xanthan gum, and pumpkin pie spice; set aside. In small bowl, combine ground flaxseeds with almond milk; set aside. In stand-up mixer, beat eggs, Swerve, melted coconut oil, agave, and liquid stevia and mix well. Add in flaxseed mixture and blend. Add pumpkin and mix until well combined.

Slowly add in prepared dry mixture to wet mixture until just combined. Allow batter sit for 10 minutes while gluten-free flour soaks up extra liquid.

Pour batter into prepared loaf pan using a spray-oiled spatula to scrape the bowl. Bake for 60 minutes or until a wooden toothpick inserted into the center comes out clean. Cool on wire rack for 10 minutes and then remove from pan and cool completely on wire rack.

Yield: 1 **LOAF**

zucchini bread with icing

A sweet, moist vegetable bread for everyday breakfast or dessert.

BREAD

1½ cups all-purpose
gluten-free flour

1 teaspoon baking soda

1 teaspoon gluten-free
baking powder

1 teaspoon xanthan gum

½ teaspoon nutmeg

¼ cup ground flaxseeds

½ cup unsweetened almond milk

1 large omega-3 egg

¾ cup Swerve

¼ cup extra-virgin
coconut oil, melted

½ cup agave

2 droppers Liquid Stevia
Lemon Drops

1 cup finely shredded zucchini

½ cup walnuts, chopped

ICING

¾ cup confectioners' Swerve

2 teaspoons unsweetened
almond milk

1 dropper Liquid Stevia
Vanilla Crème

2 teaspoons light agave

For Bread: Preheat oven to 350 degrees. Spray-oil an 8x4x2-inch loaf pan and line with parchment paper; set aside.

Sift together flour, baking soda, baking powder, xanthan gum, and nutmeg; set aside. In small bowl, combine ground flaxseeds with almond milk; set aside. In stand-up mixer, add eggs, Swerve, melted coconut oil, agave, and liquid stevia and mix well. Add in flaxseed mixture and blend. Add shredded zucchini and mix until well combined. Stir in walnuts.

Slowly add dry mixture to wet mixture until just combined. Allow batter sit for 10 minutes while gluten-free flour and quinoa flakes soak up extra liquid.

Pour batter into prepared loaf pan using a spray-oiled spatula to scrape the bowl. Bake for 60 minutes or until a wooden toothpick inserted into the center comes out clean. Cool on wire rack for 10 minutes and then remove from pan and cool completely on wire rack.

For Icing: In stand-up mixer with paddle attachment, mix the confectioners' Swerve, almond milk, liquid stevia, and agave until well combined. Beat icing for 2–3 minutes until glossy. Top zucchini bread with icing when cooled.

Yield: 1 **LOAF**

banana bread

A banana bread that can be eaten for dessert or breakfast.

1½ cups all-purpose gluten-free flour

½ cup arrowroot

½ teaspoon baking soda

½ teaspoon gluten-free baking powder

½ teaspoon xanthan gum

2 ripe bananas

⅓ cup unsweetened chunky applesauce

½ cup Swerve

3 tablespoons agave

3 tablespoons extra-virgin coconut oil, melted

1 tablespoon vanilla

1 large omega-3 egg, beaten

½ cup walnuts, chopped

Preheat oven to 350 degrees. Spray-oil an 8x8-inch baking pan and flour dust with gluten-free flour; set aside.

In mixing bowl, combine gluten-free flour, arrowroot, baking soda, baking powder, and xanthan gum; set aside.

In medium bowl, smash bananas with a fork. Work in applesauce until combined with bananas. Add Swerve, agave, melted coconut oil, vanilla, and beaten egg and stir until well combined. Slowly add dry flour mixture to wet mixture and stir until well combined. Stir in chopped nuts until just combined.

Pour batter into prepared baking pan using a spray-oiled spatula to scrape the bowl. Bake for 30–35 minutes or until a wooden toothpick inserted into the middle comes out clean. Cool on a wire rack.

Yield: 1 **LOAF**

carob corn bread

A breakfast bread or snack made with corn, yam, and carob.

2 omega-3 eggs, beaten

5 ounces Greek-style nonfat plain yogurt

1 tablespoon vanilla extract

2 droppers Liquid Stevia Cinnamon

¼ cup unsweetened almond milk

½ cup agave

½ cup Swerve

1 cup baked yam

2 teaspoons cinnamon

¾ cup cornmeal

⅓ cup roasted carob powder

⅔ cup brown rice flour

⅔ cup all-purpose gluten-free flour

1 teaspoon baking soda

1 teaspoon gluten-free baking powder

1 teaspoon xanthan gum

Preheat oven to 350 degrees. Spray-oil an 8x8-inch glass baking dish and dust with gluten-free flour; set aside.

In food processor, blend beaten eggs, yogurt, vanilla, liquid stevia, almond milk, agave, Swerve, and yam. In medium mixing bowl, combine cinnamon, cornmeal, carob, brown rice flour, gluten-free flour, baking soda, baking powder, and xanthan gum.

Pour prepared dry mixture into wet mixture in food processor. Pulse until just combined.

Pour batter into prepared baking dish using a spray-oiled spatula to scrape the bowl. Bake for 35–40 minutes or until a wooden toothpick inserted into the middle comes out clean. Cool on a wire rack.

Yield: **16 PIECES**

it's a piece of corn cake

A sweet, gluten–free Mexican corn bread spiced with cumin.

2 omega-3 eggs, beaten

5 ounces plain nonfat Greek-style yogurt

¼ cup unsweetened almond milk

1 dropper Liquid Stevia Lemon Drops or Clear flavor

3 tablespoons light agave

2 teaspoons lemon zest

½ cup dry polenta or cornmeal

½ cup quinoa flakes

½ cup quinoa flour

1 teaspoon gluten-free baking powder

½ teaspoon baking soda

1½ teaspoons Stevia Plus Powder

½ teaspoon cumin

dash of sea salt

Preheat oven to 350 degrees. Spray-oil an 8x8-inch glass baking dish and dust with quinoa flour or white rice flour; set aside.

In medium mixing bowl, whisk together beaten eggs, yogurt, almond milk, liquid stevia, agave, and lemon zest. Stir in polenta and then stir in quinoa flakes; set aside.

In small bowl, sift quinoa flour, baking powder, baking soda, Stevia Plus Powder, cumin, and salt. Add sifted dry mixture to wet mixture and mix until just combined.

Pour batter into prepared baking dish using a sray-oiled spatula to scrape the bowl. Bake on middle rack for 30 minutes or until a wooden toothpick inserted into the middle comes out clean. Cool on wire rack.

Yield: 9 PIECES

sweet hot cherry corn bread

 A dessert corn bread.

2 omega-3 eggs, beaten

5 ounces Greek-style yogurt

3 tablespoons agave

3 droppers Liquid Stevia Vanilla Crème

1 dropper Liquid Stevia Cinnamon

½ cup Swerve

½ cup unsweetened almond milk

⅓ cup quinoa flakes

⅓ cup cornmeal

1 cup plus 2 tablespoons all-purpose gluten-free flour

½ cup quinoa flour

1 teaspoon gluten-free baking powder

½ teaspoon baking soda

½ teaspoon xanthan gum

⅛ teaspoon cayenne

1½ cups (about 30) pitted cherries

½ cup chopped Brazil nuts

1 tablespoon Swerve

½ teaspoon cinnamon

Preheat oven to 350 degrees. Spray-oil an 8x8-inch glass baking dish and dust with gluten-free flour; set aside.

In large mixing bowl, whisk together beaten eggs, yogurt, agave, liquid stevias, Swerve, and almond milk. Stir in quinoa flakes and then cornmeal; set aside. In small mixing bowl, combine 1 cup flour, baking powder, baking soda, xanthan gum, and cayenne.

Add dry mixture to wet mixture and stir until just combined. Pit cherries and cut in half. Dredge cherries in remaining gluten-free flour. Add to batter and mix until just combined. In small bowl, combine Brazil nuts, Swerve, and cinnamon; set aside.

Pour batter into prepared baking dish using a spray-oiled spatula to scrape the bowl. Evenly sprinkle Brazil nut mixture on top of batter. Bake for 30–35 minutes or until a wooden toothpick inserted into the middle comes out clean. Cool on a wire rack.

Yield: **16 PIECES**

corn bread stuffing

 Make the corn bread ahead and then make the stuffing next day.

CORN BREAD

2 omega-3 eggs, beaten

5 ounces nonfat plain Greek-style yogurt

½ cup agave

¼ cup unsweetened almond milk

½ cup dry polenta or cornmeal

½ cup quinoa flakes

½ cup quinoa flour

1 teaspoon gluten-free baking powder

½ teaspoon baking soda

¼ teaspoon Celtic sea salt

1 teaspoon cumin

STUFFING

2 cups gluten-free corn bread cubes (1-inch cubes)

¼ pound butter or Earth Balance Vegetable Butter

1 cup chopped onion

1 teaspoon dried thyme

1 teaspoon dried sage

1 cup chopped parsley

1 omega-3 egg, slightly beaten

1 cup gluten-free chicken broth or vegetable broth

salt and pepper to taste

For Corn Bread: Preheat oven to 350 degrees. Spray-oil an 8x8-inch glass baking dish and dust with quinoa flour; set aside.

In large mixing bowl, whisk together beaten eggs, yogurt, agave, and almond milk. Stir in polenta and then quinoa flakes. Sift quinoa flour, baking powder, baking soda, and salt. Add sifted dry mixture to wet mixture. Blend in cumin. Pour batter into prepared baking dish using a spray-oiled spatula to scrape the bowl. Bake on middle rack for 30 minutes. Cool on wire rack.

For Stuffing: Preheat oven to 325 degrees. Cut prepared corn bread into 1-inch chunks. Place cubes on a baking sheet lined with parchment paper and bake for 20 minutes, stirring halfway through. Remove corn bread cubes from the oven and cool to room temperature.

Melt butter in pan. Sauté celery and onion until translucent. Stir in thyme, sage, and parsley. In large mixing bowl, stir corn bread and cooked onion-celery mixture together. Add beaten egg and mix well. Add the broth and mix lightly but thoroughly. Add salt and pepper to taste. Increase oven temperature to 350 degrees. Stuff the cavity of a turkey or bake the stuffing in a casserole dish at 350 degrees for 30 minutes.

eve's apple cake

A supersweet, apple-spiced breakfast bread made with egg whites and gluten-free whole grains.

1 cup egg whites

½ ripe banana

½ cup unsweetened chunky applesauce

1 Fuji apple, sliced

1 tablespoon lemon juice

1 teaspoon cinnamon

1 teaspoon pumpkin pie spice

1 teaspoon vanilla

¼ cup organic raw tahini, unsalted

2 tablespoons ground golden flaxseeds

2 droppers Liquid Stevia Vanilla Crème

2 tablespoons dark agave

1 cup quinoa flakes

1 cup quinoa flour

1 teaspoon gluten-free baking powder

½ teaspoon baking soda

½ teaspoon xanthan gum

Preheat oven to 350 degrees. Lightly spray-oil a glass 8x8-inch baking dish and dust with quinoa flour; set aside.

In food processor, purée egg whites, banana, applesauce, Fuji apple, lemon juice, cinnamon, pumpkin pie spice, vanilla, tahini, flaxseeds, liquid stevia, and agave.

In small bowl, blend quinoa flakes, quinoa flour, baking powder, baking soda, and xanthan gum. Slowly add dry ingredients to wet mixture and pulse until just combined. Let stand a few minutes so that the quinoa flakes absorb all the liquid.

Scrape out mixture with a spray-oiled spatula into prepared baking dish. Bake for 35–40 minutes or until a wooden toothpick inserted into the middle comes out clean. Cool on wire rack.

Yield: 9 PIECES

blueberry breakfast bread

A sweet breakfast bread that is low in calories and high in whole-grain fiber and protein.

1 cup egg whites

4 tablespoons light agave

2 tablespoons lemon juice

½ cup unsweetened applesauce

2 droppers Liquid Stevia Clear

1 teaspoon cinnamon

½ cup quinoa flakes

½ cup buckwheat groats

½ cup plus 2 teaspoons quinoa flour

1 teaspoon gluten-free baking powder

½ teaspoon baking soda

½ teaspoon xanthan gum

1 cup blueberries, fresh or frozen

Preheat oven to 350 degrees. Spray-oil an 8x8-inch glass baking dish and flour with quinoa flour; set aside.

In medium bowl, whisk together egg whites, agave, lemon juice, applesauce, liquid stevia, and cinnamon. Stir in quinoa flakes. Allow mixture to stand for 3–4 minutes and soak up the liquid.

In coffee grinder or blender, grind buckwheat groats until powdered. In small bowl, sift together ground buckwheat groats, quinoa flour, baking powder, baking soda, and xanthan gum. Add dry ingredients to wet mixture and blend until just combined.

Carefully dredge blueberries in remaining quinoa flour and add to wet mixture, blending until just combined. With a spray-oiled spatula, scrape out mixture into prepared baking dish. Bake for 30–35 minutes or until a wooden toothpick inserted into the middle comes out clean. Cool on wire rack.

Yield: **16 PIECES**

chocolate gingerbread

This chocolate ginger breakfast bread tastes like a winter spiced chocolate cake.

1 cup soaked buckwheat groats
(See note on soaking)

½ cup baked yam, with skin

1 teaspoon fresh minced ginger

4 droppers Liquid Stevia
Chocolate

3 tablespoons dark agave

2 omega-3 eggs

2 teaspoons cinnamon

½ teaspoon powdered ginger

3 rounded tablespoons
roasted carob

1 rounded tablespoon raw cacao

½ cup plus 2 tablespoons
unsweetened almond milk

¼ cup quinoa flour

1 teaspoon gluten-free
baking powder

½ teaspoon baking soda

1 teaspoon xanthan gum

¼ cup raw cacao nibs (optional)

Soaking Note: Start the day before. Soak ¾ cup buckwheat groats in 2 cups filtered water overnight in the refrigerator. When soaking is complete, the oats will measure 1 cup. Drain off the extra liquid.

Preheat oven to 350 degrees. Spray-oil an 8x8-inch glass baking dish and dust bottom of dish with quinoa flour or white rice flour; set aside.

In food processor, purée yam, fresh ginger, drained buckwheat groats, liquid stevia, agave, eggs, cinnamon, powdered ginger, carob, and cacao. Through spout in food processor, slowly add almond milk and continue to purée until fully blended.

In small bowl, sift together quinoa flour, baking powder, baking soda, and xanthan gum. Add dry mixture to wet mixture in food processor and purée until just combined. Add cacao nibs if desired and pulse a few times to combine.

With a spray-oiled spatula, scrape out mixture and pour into prepared baking dish. Bake for 30–35 minutes or until a wooden toothpick inserted into the middle comes out clean. Cool on wire rack.

Yield: **16 PIECES**

the other white loaf

A homemade sugar-free, wheat-free, gluten-free white sandwich bread.

1 cup white rice flour

1 cup all-purpose gluten-free flour

½ cup potato starch

½ cup tapioca starch

2 teaspoons xanthan gum

2¼ tablespoons active dry yeast

¼ teaspoon salt

3 tablespoons ground golden flaxseeds

3 omega-3 eggs

2 tablespoons Swerve or ZSweet

¼ cup grapeseed oil

1 teaspoon apple cider vinegar

1 cup unsweetened soy milk or almond milk

Lightly spray-oil an 8½x4½-inch bread pan and line with parchment paper. Sprinkle 2 tablespoons ground flaxseeds on bottom of paper; set aside.

In stand-up mixer, sift together white rice flour, gluten-free flour, potato starch, tapioca starch, xanthan gum, yeast, and salt. Mix in remaining 1 tablespoon ground flaxseeds.

In separate bowl, whisk together eggs, Swerve or ZSweet, oil, vinegar, and milk. With paddle attachment on low, slowly pour wet ingredients into dry ingredients and beat on high for 3 minutes.

Using a spray-oiled spatula, scrape down sides of bowl. Spray-oil your spatula again and spoon dough into prepared bread pan. Smooth top with oiled fingers or spray-oiled spatula. Cover with spray-oiled plastic wrap. Let rise in a warm place until dough reaches top of pan, about 2 hours.

Preheat over to 350 degrees. Cover dough in baking pan with foil tent. Bake on middle rack for 35 minutes. Take out of oven and remove foil tent. Lift bread out of pan and bake on parchment for another 3–5 minutes. Bread is done when golden and hollow sounding when tapped. Remove parchment. Cool on wire rack.

Yield: 1 LOAF

bean town brown bread

 A brown bread made with black beans and quinoa. Travels well on camping trips.

1 cup quinoa flour

3 teaspoons Stevia Plus Powder

½ teaspoon gluten-free baking powder

1 teaspoon baking soda

½ teaspoon salt

2 teaspoons cinnamon

½ teaspoon allspice

½ cup cornmeal

¾ cup organic black beans, drained

½ cup baked yam with skin

3 tablespoons roasted carob

4 tablespoons dark agave

1 cup buttermilk or unsweetened soy or almond milk

½ cup raisins dredged

1 tablespoon gluten-free flour

Spray-oil three clean, empty 15-ounce fruit or vegetable cans and dust with gluten-free flour; set aside.

In medium bowl, sift together quinoa flour, Stevia Plus Powder, baking powder, baking soda, salt, cinnamon, and allspice. Stir in cornmeal; set aside.

In food processor, purée beans, yam, carob, and agave. Add buttermilk slowly through spout in food processor. Add dry ingredients and pulse until mixed. In small bowl, dredge raisins in gluten-free flour. Add to food processor and pulse to combine. Spoon batter into prepared cans, leaving at least 2 inches from top of can for breathing room. Cover with a double piece of oiled foil, dull side up, and tie foil with twine or rubber band.

Put a rack or open metal vegetable steamer in an 8-quart soup pot and fill halfway with water. Place cans on top of rack or metal steamer. Bring water to a boil and lower to a simmer. Cover pot and steam for 2 hours. Check water level often and add more water when needed.

Remove cans and take foil off. When cans are cool enough to handle, tip upside down and bread will slide out. Cool on wire rack.

Yield: **3 LOAVES**

cinnamon twist and shout roll-ups

A sugar-free, wheat-free, gluten-free cinnamon breakfast bun with a sweet vanilla glaze.

DOUGH

2 cups all-purpose gluten-free flour

1 cup potato flour

¼ cup tapioca starch

3 teaspoons Stevia Plus Powder

1 teaspoon gluten-free baking powder

1½ tablespoons dry active yeast

½ teaspoon salt

3 tablespoons grapeseed oil

1 teaspoon vanilla extract

1 large omega-3 egg

1 cup unsweetened soy or almond milk

1–2 tablespoons water for moistening dough, if needed

FILLING

⅓ cup light agave

4 tablespoons all-purpose gluten-free flour

2 teaspoons cinnamon

2 large organic Fuji apples, chopped

1 tablespoon plus 2 teaspoons lemon juice

1½ cups organic walnuts

For Dough: In stand-up mixer, sift together gluten-free flour, potato flour, tapioca starch, Stevia Plus Powder, baking powder, yeast, and salt.

In separate bowl, whisk together the oil, vanilla, egg, and milk. In stand-up mixer with a paddle attachment on low, add wet mixture to dry mixture until a loose dough forms. Let the dough rest for 10 minutes to allow the gluten-free flour to fully absorb the liquid.

Knead the dough for a few minutes. Add 1–2 tablespoons water if the dough feels firm or dry. Grease hands with grapeseed oil and place the dough in a bowl greased with grapeseed oil, turning to coat. Cover the bowl with spray-oiled plastic wrap, and let the dough rise in a warm place for about 2 hours.

For Filling: In food processor, purée agave, flour, cinnamon, apples, lemon juice, and walnuts for 10 seconds to make a filling that can be spread evenly onto rolled-out dough.

For Assembly: Preheat oven to 350 degrees. Line a baking sheet with parchment paper. Gently deflate the risen dough and turn it out onto parchment or wax paper lightly floured with white rice flour. Fold dough over once or twice to remove the excess gas. If dough is a bit dry, add 1–2 tablespoons water to hands and knead dough a few times. Divide the dough into quarters. Roll the first quarter into a 6x10-inch rectangle. Spread ¼ of the filling over the rolled-out dough. Leave ½-inch margins. Starting with left-hand long side, roll dough into a log, sealing edge underneath with a little water on your fingers. Use a sharp, serrated knife to cut log in six 1½-inch rounds. Place rounds, seam side down, side-by-side on prepared baking sheet. Repeat this process with remaining dough and filling.

Place large piece of foil under baking sheet and fold up over edges of pastry to avoid burning. Bake for 30–35 minutes. Cool on wire rack for at least 1 hour.

GLAZE

⅓ cup light agave

4 tablespoons Swerve

1 teaspoon vanilla

3 tablespoons heavy cream or
unsweetened soy or almond milk

1 teaspoon kuzu or cornstarch
dissolved in 1 tablespoon water

For Glaze: In small saucepan, whisk together agave, Swerve, vanilla, and cream and heat to just under a slight boil. Add dissolved kuzu or cornstarch. Stir constantly for the next 5 minutes. Remove from heat and let cool. Drizzle glaze over cooled cinnamon rolls.

Yield: 24 ROLLS

wicked awesome peanut butter waffles

A healthy Sunday breakfast waffle with a bold peanut butter taste.

2¼ cups all-purpose gluten-free flour

4 teaspoons gluten-free baking powder

1 teaspoon xanthan gum

2 omega-3 eggs, beaten

2¼ cups unsweetened almond milk

1 dropper Liquid Stevia Vanilla Crème

3 tablespoons light agave

¼ cup butter or vegetable spread, melted

¾ cup organic creamy peanut butter

¼ teaspoon fine Celtic sea salt

Preheat waffle iron. When hot, lightly spray-oil.

While waffle iron is heating, sift together flour, baking powder, and xanthan gum and add to stand-up mixer. With paddle attachment, beat slowly while adding beaten eggs, almond milk, Stevia, agave, and melted vegetable spread. Scrape down sides of bowl. Continue to beat in peanut butter and salt until batter is smooth.

Pour a ladleful onto waffle iron and cook until golden, about 4 minutes. Serve immediately with Strawberry Slam Jam (page 93) and fresh sliced banana or Banana Chips (see below).

For Banana Chips: Thinly slice two ripe, organic bananas. The thinner the better—they will dehydrate faster. Place on mesh trays and dehydrate at 105 degrees for 8 hours or until desired crispness is achieved. The chips can be served whole as a snack or blended slightly in a mini-food processor and sprinkled on top of jam and waffles.

Yield: **6—7 WAFFLES**

strawberry slam jam

A fruit jam that can be used as a topping for pancakes and yogurt.

2½ cups sliced strawberries

½ cup spiced apple cider

1 teaspoon finely grated lemon zest

1 tablespoon lemon juice

2 tablespoons light agave

2 droppers Liquid Stevia Clear

2 tablespoons kuzu dissolved in ¼ cup water

....

Note: You can also use blueberries, mangoes, apricots, and raspberries. Frozen fruit may also be used.

Place sliced strawberries in food processor. Pour in cider, lemon zest, lemon juice, agave, and liquid stevia. Purée at high speed.

In medium saucepan, pour in fruit mixture and stir over a medium heat. Slowly whisk in dissolved kuzu until it disappears. Stirring constantly, cook fruit mixture down until thick, about 10 minutes.

Yield: **2 CUPS**

star buckwheat pancakes

A sugar-free, gluten-free, high-protein pancake that makes a great preworkout snack.

1 cup buckwheat groats

1 cup egg whites

½ ripe banana

2 droppers Liquid Stevia Vanilla Crème

½ cup unsweetened almond milk

1 teaspoon cinnamon

In coffee grinder, grind buckwheat groats until fine. In a blender, purée egg whites, ground buckwheat groats, banana, liquid stevia, almond milk, and cinnamon. Pour pancake batter onto spray-oiled griddle or nonstick frying pan over medium-low heat. Cook for several minutes on each side until golden brown around edges. Reduce heat gradually throughout cooking process so egg whites will not burn.

Yield: **8** PANCAKES

pumpkin spice pancakes

A high-protein, low-fat pancake made with yam that can be eaten as a dessert, snack, or breakfast.

½ cup buckwheat groats

1 cup egg whites

1 cup baked yam

3 tablespoons unsweetened almond milk

1 teaspoon pumpkin pie spice

2 droppers Liquid Stevia Cinnamon

In coffee grinder, grind buckwheat groats until fine. In a blender, purée egg whites, ground buckwheat groats, yam, almond milk, pumpkin pie spice, and liquid stevia. Pour pancake batter onto sprayed-oiled griddle or nonstick frying pan over medium-low heat. Cook for several minutes on each side until golden brown around edges. Reduce heat when needed.

Yield: 12 PANCAKES

vegan blueberry pancakes

An eggless pancake sweetened with agave, banana, and blueberries.

2 ripe bananas

2 droppers Liquid Stevia Vanilla Crème

3 tablespoons light agave

½ cup unsweetened almond milk

1 tablespoon ground golden flaxseeds

2 tablespoons water

1 cup plus 2 teaspoons all-purpose gluten-free flour

½ cup gluten-free rolled oats

2 teaspoons gluten-free baking powder

1 teaspoon cinnamon

1 cup frozen blueberries

In food processor, blend bananas, liquid stevia, agave, and almond milk. In small cup, combine ground flaxseeds and water to make a paste. Add flaxseed mixture to food processor and blend. In small bowl, combine gluten-free flour, gluten-free oats, baking powder, and cinnamon.

Add dry mixture to wet mixture in food processor. Pulse until just combined. Scrape out batter into large mixing bowl.

In separate small bowl, dredge frozen blueberries in remaining flour. Stir frozen blueberries into batter until just combined. Using ladle, spoon ¼ cup of mixture onto a spray-oiled hot griddle. Cook 3–4 minutes on each side. Cool on wire rack.

Yield: **12 PANCAKES**

queen quinoa

A gluten-free, gourmet breakfast that has high protein and stays with you all morning.

½ cup unsweetened
apple cider or juice

½ cup water

⅓ cup quinoa flakes

½ teaspoon Stevia Plus Powder

1 teaspoon pumpkin pie spice
or cinnamon

½ cup strawberries, sliced

2 teaspoons unsweetened coconut

1 tablespoon almonds, sliced

splash of unsweetened almond milk
or hemp milk

In medium saucepan, bring apple cider and water to a boil. Add quinoa flakes, Stevia Plus Powder, and pumpkin pie spice or cinnamon. At a low boil stirring constantly, cook for 90 seconds to 2 minutes or until liquid is combined.

Transfer cooked quinoa to a medium cereal bowl. Garnish with strawberries, coconut, almonds, and a splash of almond milk.

Yield: 1 SERVING

koo koo cocoa cereal

 A chocolate/carob cereal made with sprouted buckwheat and puffed rice.

3 cups sprouted buckwheat groats
(See sprouting note)

½ cup dark agave

¼ cup unsweetened almond milk

4 droppers Liquid Stevia
Dark Chocolate

2 tablespoons raw cacao

2 tablespoons roasted carob powder

¼ teaspoon cinnamon

3 cups unsweetened puffed rice

½ cup dry-roasted
almonds, chopped

Sprouting Note: Start soaking and sprouting the buckwheat groats several days before. In a covered container, soak 2 cup raw buckwheat groats in 5 cups filtered water overnight in the refrigerator. In the morning, drain groats into a large colander and spread the groats evenly around the sides with a flat spatula. Place a plate underneath the colander to catch dripping water. Cover the colander with a paper towel and let the groats sprout on the counter, out of the sun in a cool, dry place, for 36–48 hours. When you see a little white tail pop out of the groats, sprouting is complete. Place sprouted groats in a container and refrigerate until ready to use. Measure 3 cups of sprouted buckwheat groats for recipe.

In large bowl, mix agave, almond milk, and liquid stevia. Whisk in cacao, carob, and cinnamon until smooth. In separate bowl, pour ¼ cup of wet cocoa mixture on top of puffed rice.

Add ¼ cup of chopped nuts to puffed rice mixture. Toss and place immediately on Teflex sheet, spreading mixture evenly and as flat as possible for even dehydration.

In second mixing bowl, place sprouted buckwheat and pour in the rest of the wet cacao mixture. Add the remaining almonds and toss. Transfer batter onto second Teflex sheet, spreading evenly.

Dehydrate both sheets of cereal at 105 degrees. The puffed rice will dehydrate faster than buckwheat, so pull out the puffed rice at 8 hours. The buckwheat will dry for 16 hours. When both trays are done, transfer to a large bowl and mix the two cereals together, breaking up the buckwheat into bite-size pieces. Scoop out a cupful into a cereal bowl and splash with your choice of milk.

Store in an airtight container. Cereal will keep for 30 days.

Yield: **6—7 CUPS**

great low-fat vanilla granola

A gluten-free granola made with sprouted buckwheat, goji berries, raisins, and agave.

2 cups sprouted buckwheat groats
(See sprouting note)

½ cup raisins

¼ cup goji berries

4 tablespoons agave

1 teaspoon vanilla

2 droppers Liquid Stevia
Vanilla Crème

1 teaspoon cinnamon
or pumpkin pie spice

....

Sprouting Note: Start soaking and sprouting the buckwheat groats several days before. In a covered container, soak 1 cup raw buckwheat groats in 2½ cups filtered water overnight in the refrigerator. In the morning, drain groats into a large colander. You may use the buckwheat groats soaked, or continue to sprout. To sprout, spread the groats evenly around the sides with a flat spatula. Place a plate underneath the colander to catch dripping water. Cover the colander with a paper towel and let the groats sprout on the counter, out of the sun in a cool, dry place, for 36–48 hours. When you see a little white tail pop out of the groats, sprouting is complete. Place sprouted groats in a container and refrigerate until ready to use. Measure 2 cups of sprouted buckwheat groats for recipe.

Mix sprouted buckwheat groats, raisins, goji berries, agave, vanilla, liquid stevia, and cinnamon or pumpkin pie spice. Stir until all ingredients are mixed well and spread onto dehydrator sheet. Dehydrate at 105 degrees for 12–16 hours.

Store in an airtight container. Cereal will keep for 30 days.

Yield: **3–4 CUPS DRY GRANOLA**

raw hemp protein bars

 A nutrient-dense hemp protein bar made with hemp butter, raw cacao, goji berries, and agave.

½ cup buckwheat groats

1½ cups filtered water

¼ cup raw cacao nibs

¼ cup ground goji berries

½ cup raw hemp butter

2 droppers Liquid Stevia Chocolate

1½ tablespoons organic vanilla

1 teaspoon cinnamon

4 tablespoons dark agave

½ cup coconut-date rolls

¼ cup raw almonds

2 rounded tablespoons hemp protein powder

¼ cup roasted carob powder

½ cup plus 3 tablespoons hempseeds

¼ cup unsweetened almond milk

Soak ½ cup buckwheat groats in 1½ cups water overnight, drain well, and pat dry with a paper towel. The buckwheat groats will have expanded to over ½ cup, but still use all the buckwheat.

In food processor, purée cacao nibs, goji berries, hemp butter, liquid stevia, vanilla, cinnamon, agave, coconut-date rolls, almonds, hemp protein powder, carob, and hempseeds. Add almond milk slowly through the spout of food processor and continue processing.

Scrape down sides of food processor and purée until the batter is a thick, well-blended dough. Add a little extra almond milk if needed. Test batter to make sure it can be easily handled and molded into bars without sticking to your fingers. If you need to make it less sticky, add more carob.

Scoop batter out and place in mixing bowl. Fold in ½ cup of hempseeds by pressing mixture against the side of the bowl with the back of a spatula. Place batter on a sheet of wax paper and mold into a flat log shape. Cut into ½-inch bars. Roll bars in extra hempseeds.

Place rolled hemp bars on Teflex dehydrator sheet and dehydrate for 18–20 hours at 105 degrees. Halfway through the dehydrating time, use a spatula to remove bars from Teflex sheet, remove Teflex sheet, and place bars opposite side up on mesh screens for the rest of the time. The bars will dry all the way through. Dehydrating time may vary depending upon how chewy you want your bars.

Yield: **12 BARS**

gluten-free blueberry oat bars

A chewy blueberry bar with lemon zest and gluten-free rolled oats.

CRUST

½ cup raw buckwheat groats

1½ cups water

½ cup all-purpose
gluten-free flour

¼ teaspoon baking soda

1 teaspoon cinnamon

1 cup gluten-free rolled oats

¼ cup almond meal

4 tablespoons butter or
Earth Balance 50/50 sticks, chilled

2 tablespoons lemon juice

FILLING

1½ cups dried blueberries

⅔ cup plain nonfat
Greek-style yogurt

½ cup Swerve

¼ cup agave

2 teaspoons vanilla

2 droppers Liquid Stevia
Cinnamon

2 tablespoons all-purpose
gluten-free flour

1 teaspoon lemon zest

1 large egg white, lightly beaten

For Crust: Start the day before. Soak buckwheat groats in water in a covered container overnight in the refrigerator. Drain buckwheat groats thoroughly; set aside.

Preheat oven to 325 degrees. Spray-oil an 8x8-inch baking dish; set aside.

In food processor, add the drained buckwheat groats, flour, baking soda, and cinnamon and pulse 10 times to begin to break down soaked buckwheat groats. Add gluten-free oats, almond meal, chilled butter, and lemon juice to food processor. Pulse 7–8 times then switch to purée and blend until crust forms a ball.

Reserve ½ cup of oat mixture; set aside. Press remaining oat mixture into the bottom of prepared 8x8-inch baking dish, spreading crust evenly to about a ½-inch thick.

For Filling: Combine blueberries, yogurt, Swerve, agave, vanilla, liquid stevia, flour, lemon zest, and beaten egg white. Spread blueberry mixture over prepared crust. Sprinkle reserved oat mixture evenly over filling. Bake for 40–45 minutes or until edges are golden. Cool on wire rack.

Yield: **24 BARS**

raw cherry pistachio seed bars

A chewy cherry bar with omega-3 hemp, pumpkin seeds, and pistachios.

1 cup raw almonds, soaked

¼ cup raw pumpkin seeds, soaked

¼ cup flaxseeds, soaked

1½ cups frozen pitted cherries

1½ tablespoons kuzu

½ cup agave

1 teaspoon cinnamon

1 teaspoon vanilla

¼ teaspoon Himalayan salt

½ cup raw pistachios

½ cup raw cacao nibs

Start the day before. In bowl covered with lid, soak raw almonds, pumpkin seeds, and flaxseeds in 3 cups filtered water in refrigerator overnight. Drain and pat dry; set aside.

In food processor, blend frozen cherries and kuzu until creamy. Add soaked almonds, pumpkin seeds, and flaxseeds to food processor and process until well blended. Add agave, cinnamon, vanilla, and salt to food processor and blend until just combined.

Transfer prepared cherry mixture to a mixing bowl. Stir in pistachios and cacao nibs.

Spread batter onto Teflex dehydrating sheet and shape into a 10x10-inch square about ½-inch high.

Dehydrate at 105 degrees for 10–12 hours. Carefully peel bar batter off of Teflex sheet, flip over, and place on mesh sheet and continue to dehydrate for another 8–9 hours. Cut or break into bars. Store in an airtight container.

Yield: **16 PIECES**

muffins, scones, and bagels

Many of the sweet breakfast breads from the previous chapter can be made into muffins. Pour the sweet bread batter into prepared muffin trays, then bake the muffins for 20 minutes or until a wooden toothpick inserted into the middle comes out clean.

Silicone muffin molds or individual silicone cupcake molds are the best baking tools for a sugar-free, gluten-free muffin that doesn't stick to the sides of muffin tins or liners. If you have to use liners and tins, use foil liners rather than paper liners.

If the batter is light colored, you can use a foil tent over the muffins to ensure they don't over-brown and bake all the way through. To make a foil tent, fold a large piece of aluminum foil into fours and cut a semicircle four inches from the end of the folded corner. Open up the foil to create a large circle and tent it over prepared batter in silicone muffin molds or tins. Use foil tents over muffins the last 5 minutes of baking if necessary.

Some of my favorite muffins are Courageous Carrot Cake Muffins that use fresh carrot juice and can be topped with Cream Cheese Frosting or Vegan Cream Cheese Frosting. Maui Muffins are a tribute to my trip to Maui where I saw the island's desserts using the fresh tastes of the tropics: pineapple, coconut, and mango.

Scones are a tribute to my semester abroad in Edinburgh, Scotland, and also to my addiction to Starbucks' maple-glazed scones, which I do not eat anymore (I look, but I don't touch). The scone recipes I make are easy spoon-dropped scones like Carob Chip Scones or fruity nut scones called Cran-Orange Pistachio Scones, which are patted into an 8-inch circle and cut into wedges. A spray-oiled knife is a gluten-free kitchen technique that allows you to cut through gluten-free dough without the knife sticking.

Bagels were and forever will be my favorite way to eat gluten-free bread. I chose to add Wholly Cinnamon Raisin Bagels to the cookbook because that is what I always used to eat when I lived in Boston. That recipe can be altered very easily into Plain Bagels and Sesame Bagels by eliminating the cinnamon and raisins or rolling the outside of the freshly boiled bagels in sesame seeds. Either way, a whole bagel can be split in half and toasted to reduce the starch. Even though these recipes are gluten-free and sugar-free, they still contain carbohydrates. It's better to share a whole bagel than to eat one alone!

BREAK THE FAST MUFFINS

COURAGEOUS CARROT CAKE MUFFINS

BLUEBERRY CORN BREAD MUFFINS

LEMON POPPY SEED MUFFINS

MAUI MUFFINS

MAGIC MUFFINS WITH GREAT GANACHE

CAROB CHIP SCONES

CRAN-ORANGE PISTACHIO SCONES

WHOLLY CINNAMON RAISIN BAGELS

break the fast muffins

 A sweet gluten-free carob muffin made with high-protein flours, buckwheat groats, and agave.

2 omega-3 eggs

½ cup plain nonfat Greek-style yogurt

2 tablespoons grapeseed oil

½ cup unsweetened applesauce

½ cup carob powder

½ cup buckwheat groats

⅓ cup quinoa flakes

¾ cup quinoa flour

2 teaspoons Stevia Plus Powder

1 teaspoon cinnamon

1 teaspoon gluten-free baking powder

½ teaspoon baking soda

1 teaspoon xanthan gum

¾ cup unsweetened carob chips (See dairy-free note)

Dairy-Free Note: Carob chips may contain whey from dairy, so for a substitute, use ½ cup raw cacao nibs.

Preheat oven to 350 degrees. Line muffin tins with foil liners or spray-oil silicone muffin trays; set aside.

In stand-up mixer with paddle attachment, beat eggs. Add yogurt, oil, and applesauce and mix well. Add in carob powder and blend; set aside.

To grind buckwheat groats, place in a coffee grinder or blender and grind until fine. Place ground groats in a small bowl. With a fork or small whisk, mix in quinoa flakes, quinoa flour, Stevia Plus Powder, cinnamon, baking powder, baking soda, and xanthan gum.

Slowly add dry mixture to wet mixture in stand-up mixing bowl. Set aside for a few minutes so that the quinoa flakes can absorb the rest of the liquid. Stir in carob chips.

Spoon batter into prepared muffin trays to about three-quarters of the way full. Bake for 25–30 minutes or until a wooden toothpick inserted into the center of a muffin comes out clean. Cool on wire rack.

Yield: **12 MEDIUM MUFFINS**

courageous carrot cake muffins

Awesome carrot muffins with plump, spicy raisins.

½ cup unsweetened applesauce

1 tablespoon lemon juice

½ cup fresh carrot juice

4 droppers Liquid Stevia Clear

2 droppers Liquid Stevia Vanilla Crème

½ cup raisins

1 teaspoon pumpkin pie spice

1 teaspoon cinnamon

4 teaspoons arrowroot

2 omega-3 eggs

1 tablespoon grapeseed oil

4 tablespoons agave

1 cup grated carrots

1 cup quinoa flour

¾ cup quinoa flakes

1 teaspoon baking soda

1 teaspoon gluten-free baking powder

1 teaspoon xanthan gum

Preheat oven to 350 degrees. Line muffin tin with foil liners or spray-oil silicone muffin trays; set aside.

Over medium heat in a medium saucepan, combine applesauce, lemon juice, ¼ cup of carrot juice, liquid stevias, raisins, pumpkin pie spice, and cinnamon until just under a boil. In small cup, whisk 2 teaspoons arrowroot in remaining ¼ cup of carrot juice until dissolved and add to saucepan. Cook down liquid, stirring constantly for another 10 minutes or until a wooden spoon can clear the bottom of the saucepan.

In stand-up mixer with paddle attachment, beat eggs, oil, and agave. Stir in grated carrots. Add reduced carrot juice mixture and blend.

In small bowl, mix the quinoa flour, quinoa flakes, baking soda, baking powder, xanthan gum, and remaining 2 teaspoons arrowroot.

Add dry ingredients to wet mixture and blend with paddle attachment. Let batter stand a few minutes to allow the quinoa flakes to soak in the rest of the liquid.

Spoon batter into prepared muffin trays to about three-quarters full. Bake for 25–30 minutes or until a wooden toothpick inserted into the center of the muffin comes out clean. Cool on wire rack.

Yield: 12 MEDIUM MUFFINS

blueberry corn bread muffins

A sugar-free, wheat-free, corn bread muffin with blueberries and agave.

2 omega-3 eggs

5 ounces Greek-style nonfat plain yogurt

¼ cup unsweetened almond milk

1 tablespoon vanilla extract

3 tablespoons light agave

½ cup cornmeal

½ cup quinoa flakes

½ cup quinoa flour

½ cup plus 2 teaspoons all-purpose gluten-free flour

1 teaspoon gluten-free baking powder

½ teaspoon baking soda

2 teaspoons Stevia Plus Powder

1 cup blueberries, fresh or frozen

Preheat oven to 350 degrees. Line muffin tin with foil liners or spray-oil silicone muffins trays; set aside.

In medium mixing bowl, beat eggs. Whisk in yogurt, almond milk, vanilla, and agave. Stir in cornmeal and then stir in quinoa flakes; set aside.

In small bowl, sift quinoa flour, ½ cup gluten-free flour, baking powder, baking soda, and Stevia Plus Powder. Add dry mixture to wet mixture and blend until just combined.

In separate small bowl, dredge blueberries with remaining 2 teaspoons gluten-free flour. Add dredged berries to wet mixture and gently stir.

Spoon batter into prepared muffin trays to about three-quarters full. Bake on middle rack for 30 minutes. Cool on wire rack.

Yield: 9 MUFFINS

lemon poppy seed muffins

A sweet and zesty lemon muffin with poppy seeds.

MUFFINS

1½ cups all-purpose gluten-free flour

1 teaspoon baking soda

1½ teaspoons gluten-free baking powder

½ teaspoon xanthan gum

2 tablespoons ground golden flaxseeds

½ cup unsweetened almond milk

1 large omega-3 egg

½ cup Swerve

¼ cup grape grapeseed oil

½ cup agave

3 droppers Liquid Stevia Lemon Drops

1 tablespoon lemon juice

2 teaspoons lemon zest

⅔ cup quinoa flakes

¼ cup poppy seeds

ICING

¾ cup confectioners' Swerve

2 teaspoons unsweetened almond milk

1 dropper Liquid Stevia Lemon Drops

2 teaspoons light agave

½ teaspoon lemon zest

For Muffins: Preheat oven to 350 degrees. Line muffin tin with foil liners or spray-oil silicone muffin trays; set aside.

Sift together flour, baking soda, baking powder, and xanthan gum; set aside. In small bowl, combine ground flaxseeds with almond milk; set aside. In stand-up mixer, add eggs, Swerve, grapeseed oil, agave, and liquid stevia. Mix on high for 3 minutes or until batter is frothy. Add in flaxseed mixture, lemon juice, and lemon zest and blend.

Slowly add in prepared dry mixture to wet mixture until just combined. Add in quinoa flakes and blend. Add in poppy seeds and blend. Allow batter sit for 10 minutes while gluten-free flour and quinoa flakes soak up extra liquid.

Pour batter into prepared muffin trays. Bake for 20 minutes or until a wooden toothpick inserted into the center comes out clean. Check muffins halfway through and if they are browning quickly, cover with a foil tent. Cool on a wire rack for 30 minutes and then remove from pans and cool completely.

For Icing: In stand-up mixer with paddle attachment, blend confectioners' Swerve, almond milk, liquid stevia, agave, and lemon zest. Beat icing for 2–3 minutes until glossy. When muffins are cooled, top with icing.

Yield: **12 MUFFINS**

maui muffins

A tropical sweet muffin with papaya, pineapple, and macadamia nuts.

1½ cups all-purpose gluten-free flour

1 teaspoon baking soda

1½ teaspoons gluten-free baking powder

½ teaspoon xanthan gum

1 large omega-3 egg

½ cup Swerve

¼ cup extra-virgin coconut oil, melted

½ cup agave

2 teaspoons vanilla extract

2 droppers Liquid Stevia Vanilla Crème

½ cup fresh mango

¾ cup unsweetened pineapple, crushed, drained

¾ cup macadamia nuts, chopped

1 cup unsweetened coconut

Preheat oven to 350 degrees. Line muffin tin with foil liners or spray-oil silicone muffin trays; set aside.

Sift together flour, baking soda, baking powder, and xanthan gum; set aside. In stand-up mixer, add eggs, Swerve, coconut oil, agave, vanilla, and liquid stevia. In mini-food processor, purée fresh mango. Add mango purée and pineapple to wet mixture and blend until well combined.

Slowly add in prepared dry mixture to wet mixture and mix until just combined. Allow batter sit for 10 minutes while the gluten-free flour soaks up extra liquid. Add in macadamia nuts and coconut and mix until just combined.

Pour batter into prepared muffin trays. Bake for 20 minutes or until a wooden toothpick inserted into the center comes out clean. Check muffins halfway through and if they are browning quickly, cover with a foil tent. Cool on a wire rack for 30 minutes and then remove from pans and cool completely.

Yield: 12 MUFFINS

magic muffins with great ganache

Sugar-free, wheat-free peanut butter muffins with chocolate fudge ganache topping.

MUFFINS

¾ cup butter
or vegetable butter, softened

½ cup smooth peanut butter

½ cup Swerve

1 tablespoon vanilla extract

2 droppers Liquid Stevia
Vanilla Crème

½ cup light agave

2 large omega-3 eggs

1 cup all-purpose
gluten-free flour

1 cup quinoa flour

3 teaspoons Stevia Plus Powder

2 teaspoons gluten-free
baking powder

2 teaspoons xanthan gum

½ teaspoon sea salt

¾ cup unsweetened almond milk

For Muffins: Preheat oven to 375 degrees. Line muffin tin with foil liners or spray-oil large silicone muffin trays; set aside.

In stand-up mixer, cream butter and peanut butter. Add Swerve and blend. Add vanilla, liquid stevia, and agave and beat for about 3 minutes. Add eggs one at a time and beat until smooth.

In separate bowl, sift together the gluten-free flour, quinoa flour, Stevia Plus Powder, baking powder, xanthan gum, and salt. In stand-up mixer, alternate adding dry ingredients with almond milk into wet mixture, starting and ending with dry ingredients. Scrape down sides of bowl when needed. Pour batter into prepared muffin tin almost to the top, leaving about ⅛ inch. This way the muffins will rise and be easy to dip into the ganache. Bake for 25–30 minutes or until a wooden toothpick inserted into the center of the muffin comes out clean. Cool on wire racks.

Yield: **12 LARGE MUFFINS**

GANACHE

1 cup grain-sweetened chocolate chips (See gluten-free note)

½ cup heavy cream

2 tablespoons light agave

2 droppers Liquid Stevia Chocolate

¼ cup unsalted butter or vegetable butter, softened

3 tablespoons Swerve

1 tablespoon kuzu dissolved in 2 tablespoons cold water

....

Gluten-Free Note: Grain-sweetened chocolate chips may contain malted barley, which contains gluten. For a gluten-free substitute, melt 2 ounces unsweetened baking chocolate in a double boiler over medium heat. Stir in an extra ¼ cup Swerve or ZSweet and substitute this mixture for the grain-sweetened chips. Then stir in remaining ingredients.

For Ganache: Place chips in medium bowl; set aside. In medium saucepan over medium heat, stir cream, agave, liquid stevia, butter, and Swerve until hot but just under a boil. Add dissolved kuzu and stir constantly until thick. Pour cream mixture over chocolate chips and stir until melted. Let cool completely.

When muffins have cooled, tip muffins upside down and dip into ganache. Let excess drip off before flipping right side up. Let ganache set for 10 minutes before serving. Keep muffins refrigerated.

carob chip scones

A light, gluten-free scone made with carob chips and agave.

1½ cups plus 1 tablespoon all-purpose gluten-free flour

1 cup quinoa flour

1 teaspoon gluten-free baking powder

½ teaspoon baking soda

1 teaspoon xanthan gum

1 teaspoon cinnamon

dash salt

½ cup vegetable shortening, chilled

1 omega-3 egg

¾ cup unsweetened soy milk or almond milk

1 tablespoon vanilla extract

4 tablespoons dark agave plus extra for topping

4 droppers Liquid Stevia Chocolate

2 droppers Liquid Stevia Vanilla Crème

¾ cup unsweetened carob chips (See dairy-free note)

....

Dairy-Free Note: Carob chips may contain whey from dairy, so for a substitute, use ½ cup raw cacao nibs.

Preheat ungreased baking pan in 400-degree oven.

In large mixing bowl, sift together 1½ cups gluten-free flour, quinoa flour, baking powder, baking soda, xanthan gum, cinnamon, and salt. Cut in vegetable shortening with pastry cutter or fork until flour resembles little balls the size of peas.

In separate bowl, whisk together egg, soy milk or almond milk, vanilla, agave, and liquid stevias. In stand-up mixer with paddle attachment, add wet ingredients to dry ingredients. Be careful to not overwork dough. Gluten-free dough is naturally sticky.

Dredge unsweetened carob chips in the remaining tablespoon gluten-free flour. Toss to lightly coat chips. Fold chips carefully into dough. Spoon heaping tablespoons of dough onto heated baking pan. Drizzle remaining teaspoon of dark agave on each scone in a crisscross pattern.

Lower oven heat to 350 degrees. Bake for 15–20 minutes. Cool on wire rack.

Yield: 12 SCONES

cran-orange pistachio scones

A sweet breakfast scone with crunchy topping.

2½ cups plus 1 tablespoon all-purpose gluten-free flour

1 teaspoon gluten-free baking powder

½ teaspoon baking soda

1 teaspoon xanthan gum

¼ teaspoon salt

1 cup butter or Earth Balance 50/50 sticks, chilled

1 omega-3 egg, beaten

½ cup Swerve, plus extra for topping

¼ cup agave

3 droppers Liquid Stevia Valencia Orange

2 droppers Liquid Stevia Vanilla Crème

1 teaspoon orange zest

¼ cup pistachios, chopped

½ cup unsweetened dried cranberries

1 egg white, beaten

Preheat oven to 400 degrees. Line a baking sheet with parchment paper; set aside.

In large mixing bowl, sift together 2½ cups gluten-free flour, baking powder, baking soda, xanthan gum, and salt. Cut butter into small pieces. Cut butter pieces into flour mixture with pastry cutter or fork until flour resembles little balls the size of peas.

In stand-up mixture with paddle attachment, mix together the beaten egg, Swerve, agave, and liquid stevias. Mix in orange zest. Add dry ingredients to wet ingredients and mix. Be careful to not overwork dough.

On medium heat in nonstick sauté pan, toast pistachios until oils are released, about 8 minutes. Cool nuts. Dredge cranberries in the extra tablespoon of gluten-free flour. Fold nuts and dredged cranberries into dough until just combined.

Turn dough out onto prepared baking sheet. Spray-oil hands and pat dough into an 8-inch circle. With spray-oiled knife, cut dough into 8 wedges (do not separate wedges). Brush dough with egg white. Sprinkle dough with extra Swerve. Bake for 13–15 minutes or until golden. Cool on wire rack.

Yield: **8 SCONES**

wholly cinnamon raisin bagels

A homemade, sugar-free, gluten-free, cinnamon raisin bagel.

¼ cup cornmeal

2 cups plus 1 tablespoon all-purpose gluten-free flour

½ cup white rice flour

½ cup tapioca starch

1 teaspoon Stevia Plus Powder

2 teaspoons cinnamon

½ teaspoon salt

1 tablespoon xanthan gum

1 tablespoon yeast

1 tablespoon ground golden flaxseeds

2 large egg whites

2 tablespoons light agave

2 tablespoons grapeseed oil

1 teaspoon apple cider vinegar

1 cup warm water

½ cup raisins

2 tablespoons agave

....

Note: This gluten-free dough is very sticky. Use oil generously on hands to handle dough.

....

Note: Using agave to activate yeast may not produce any fizzing. To ensure activation of the yeast, 1 teaspoon of sugar may be used instead of agave.

Line a large baking sheet with parchment paper and sprinkle cornmeal evenly on top; set aside.

In stand-up mixer, sift together 2 cups gluten-free flour, white rice flour, tapioca starch, Stevia Plus Powder, cinnamon, salt, xanthan gum, and yeast. Stir in flaxseeds.

In separate bowl, mix egg whites, agave, oil, vinegar, and warm water. Slowly add wet mixture to dry mixture in stand-up mixer with paddle attachment. Beat on high for 3–4 minutes. In small bowl, dredge raisins in remaining gluten-free flour. Gently fold in raisins into wet batter.

Spray-oil a large spatula to scrape down sides of bowl. Spray-oil a large spoon to scoop out about ⅛ of dough onto prepared baking sheet. Grease hands and shape dough into a ball. Flatten slightly with palm and using your clean and greased index finger, make a hole in the center, about the size of a pea. You may also use greased fingers to smooth out rough edges of dough.

Repeat this process with the rest of the dough until you make 8 bagels total. Lightly cover prepared bagels with a spray-oiled piece of plastic wrap. Allow bagels to rise for 1–2 hours, or until they have doubled in size.

Preheat oven to 375 degrees. In large skillet, bring 2½ inches of water to a boil. Add in 2 tablespoons agave. Once bagels have risen, drop 2 to 3 bagels in the boiling water. Boil for 30 seconds and then flip over and cook another 30 seconds. Using a flat strainer or slotted spoon, remove bagels and put back onto same baking sheet lined with parchment paper. Repeat this process with remaining bagels.

Bake for 25–30 minutes. Cool on wire rack. Serve with almond butter and agave.

Yield: **8 LARGE BAGELS**

cakes and cupcakes

The techniques for successfully making sugar-free and gluten-free cakes and cupcakes are nothing short of a culinary miracle. Eliminating sugar from a recipe takes away the ability to create volume and sweetness, hold in moisture, and caramelize the batter, which gives the perfectly baked cake its beautiful golden glow. Omitting wheat or glutenous grain flours such as barley and spelt also dramatically lessens the chance of baked goods rising, as well as having the structure, firmness, and that taste we are all too familiar with that come from white flour. Making a cake is an act of love. Making a sugar-free and gluten-free cake is an act of devotion to the tenth degree.

Now that we have discussed the ingredients that are not going into our cakes and cupcakes, let's list the ingredients that are going to create a cake that is free of processed sugar and wheat flour. Starting with the sugar alternatives, you will need: liquid stevia, Stevia Plus Powder, agave, and an erythritol, like the brand Swerve.

Liquid stevia comes in flavors, like Chocolate and Vanilla Crème, which heighten the taste of any sugar-free recipe. Stevia Plus Powder is gray stevia extract mixed with an FOS or inulin fiber. Agave adds moisture and sweetness and is low glycemic. I use the smallest amounts of agave in a recipe as possible because it is a fructose syrup from a plant and does have calories. But when agave is combined in a recipe with good fats, fiber, and protein, the fructose in agave breaks down slowly and is absorbed into the bloodstream more slowly than processed white sugar.

As a natural sweetener made from fruit and vegetable fiber, erythritol helps give volume to a recipe without any additional calories. Swerve is a product that combines erythritol and oligofructose and it has the best sweetness for cakes. Yet erythritol products do not hold moisture in baked goods like sugar does and they can dry out even the best of sugar-free baking recipes. In order to help cakes retain their moisture, I use grapeseed oil, a light, monounsaturated oil that can withstand heat and has a neutral flavor. I whisk oil, eggs, and water in a stand-up mixer for at least 5 minutes or until frothy. This helps the cake's gluten-free flours rise and gives it lightness.

The gluten-free flours used to replace white wheat flour are an all-purpose gluten-free flour, tapioca starch, potato starch, and xanthan gum. Sift these flours together before adding them to your wet mixture. Also, when shopping and setting up your pantry, look for gluten-free baking powder if you absolutely cannot have any gluten. And extracts like vanilla and almond also come gluten-free.

The best cakes to make vegan, sugar-free, and gluten-free are those made in a single glass baking dish like a carrot cake or chocolate cake. Recipes like Courageous Carrot Cake Muffins and Chocolate Carob Ginger Bread substitute as cakes that don't need much help rising like the Miami Beach Bikini Cake or Marilyn and Strawberries Cake. For example, the carrot cake muffin mixture can replace each egg using 1 ounce of silken tofu, puréed and made in an 8x8-inch glass baking dish. The carob gingerbread tastes like a chocolate cake and can be made vegan by also substituting 1 ounce of silken tofu, puréed for each egg. Other single-baking-dish cakes are Eve's Apple Cake, Blueberry Breakfast Bread, and Magic Muffins.

MIAMI BEACH BIKINI CAKE

LEMON-FILLED FUN CAKE

MARILYN AND STRAWBERRIES

VOLUPTUOUS VOLCANO CAKES

MOCHA MACA CRUMB CAKE

BLUEBERRY POUNDLESS CAKE

PINEAPPLE CARROT CAKE

CREAM CHEESE FROSTING

VEGAN CREAM CHEESE FROSTING

VANILLA BABYCAKE CUPCAKES

CHOCOLATE BABYCAKE CUPCAKES

miami beach bikini cake

This is my sugar-free, wheat-free take on a winning double-layer chocolate cake.

CAKE

(makes one 8-inch cake)

½ cup grain-sweetened chocolate chips (See gluten-free note)

2 cups all-purpose gluten-free flour

½ cup potato starch

½ cup tapioca starch

1 teaspoon gluten-free baking powder

1 teaspoon baking soda

1 teaspoon xanthan gum

2 teaspoons Stevia Plus Powder

¼ teaspoon salt

2 large omega-3 eggs

3 tablespoons grapeseed oil

3 tablespoons water

½ cup unsweetened chocolate almond milk

¾ cup Swerve

1 tablespoon vanilla

3 droppers Liquid Stevia Chocolate

Gluten-Free Note: Grain-sweetened chocolate chips may contain malted barley, which contains gluten. For a gluten-free substitute, melt 3 ounces unsweetened baking chocolate with 1 tablespoon light agave and 1 dropper liquid stevia.

For Cake: Although this cake has two layers, the ingredient list makes enough for one 8-inch cake. It's best to make the first layer and then repeat the process again for the second layer.

Preheat oven to 350 degrees. Grease and flour two 8-inch cake pans or spray-oil two 8-inch silicone pans; set aside.

In double boiler, melt chocolate chips; set aside. In medium mixing bowl, sift together gluten-free flour, potato starch, tapioca starch, baking powder, baking soda, xanthan gum, Stevia Plus Powder, and salt; set aside.

In stand-up mixer using wire attachment, beat eggs, oil, water, and chocolate almond milk until frothy, about 5 minutes. Add Swerve, vanilla, and liquid stevia. Beat well. With a spatula, add melted chips. In stand-up mixer, change to paddle attachment and add dry ingredients to wet mixture at low speed. Beat as little as possible.

Pour batter into prepared pan. Repeat cake batter recipe for second layer.

TOPPING

1 cup grain-sweetened
chocolate chips
(See gluten-free note)

1 cup chopped walnuts

½ cup agave

2 teaspoons cinnamon

2 teaspoons unsweetened
dark cocoa powder

FROSTING

1 cup heavy cream

2 tablespoons light agave

Gluten-free Note: For this recipe the gluten-free substitute must be made once for the cake and again for the topping. For topping, substitute either 1 cup unsweetened carob chips (not dairy-free) or ½ cup raw cacao nibs (dairy-free) for the grain-sweetened chocolate chips. Over medium heat in a double boiler, melt 13 ounces unsweetened baking chocolate. Stir in an extra ¼ cup Swerve or ZSweet.

For Topping: In small bowl, mix chocolate chips, walnuts, agave, cinnamon, and cocoa. Divide nut mixture in half and sprinkle evenly onto each unbaked cake layer. Bake cake 30–35 minutes or until a toothpick inserted into the middle comes out clean. Cool on wire rack until cool enough to remove from pans.

For Frosting: In stand-up mixer with wire attachment, beat heavy cream with agave until stiff, about 5 minutes. Place first cake layer on a cake dish. Frost top of first cake and sides completely. Place second cake on top and frost sides only. Leave top of cake unfrosted. Keep refrigerated.

Yield: 1 DOUBLE-LAYER CAKE

lemon-filled fun cake

Individual sugar-free, wheat-free, lemon-filled, baby Bundt cakes.

LEMON FILLING

½ cup lemon juice

1 cup water

2 tablespoons agar agar flakes

1 tablespoon lemon zest

6 tablespoons light agave

1 dropper Liquid Stevia Lemon Drops

5 tablespoons kuzu dissolved in ½ cup cold water

CAKE

2 cups all-purpose gluten-free flour

½ cup potato starch

½ cup tapioca starch

3 teaspoons Stevia Plus Powder

1 teaspoon gluten-free baking powder

1 teaspoon baking soda

1 teaspoon xanthan gum

½ teaspoon salt

2 large omega-3 eggs

3 tablespoons grapeseed oil

3 tablespoons water

½ cup unsweetened vanilla almond, rice, or soy milk

½ cup Swerve

3 droppers Liquid Stevia Lemon Drops

2 tablespoons lemon zest

lemon slices, for garnish

For Filling: Make lemon filling the day before and keep in the fridge overnight to set. In medium saucepan, whisk together lemon juice, water, agar agar flakes, lemon zest, agave, and liquid stevia. Bring to a boil and simmer until agar agar flakes is dissolved. In small cup, dissolve kuzu in cold water by stirring with a spoon and add to saucepan. Over medium-low heat, stir until thick, about 10 minutes. Transfer to a bowl. Let cool and place covered in fridge overnight.

For Cake: Preheat oven to 350 degrees. Spray-oil silicone baby Bundt pans; set aside.

Sift together gluten-free flour, potato starch, tapioca starch, Stevia Plus Powder, baking powder, baking soda, xanthan gum, and salt; set aside.

In stand-up mixer using wire attachment, beat eggs, oil, water, and milk until frothy, about 5 minutes. Mix in Swerve, liquid stevia, and lemon zest.

In stand-up mixer, change to a paddle attachment on low and add dry ingredients slowly to wet ingredients. Beat as little as possible.

Pour batter into prepared pans about three-quarters of the way full. Let sit 5 minutes before placing in oven. Bake for 30–35 minutes or until cake is firm. Transfer to wire rack immediately. Cakes will slide out easily. Cool completely.

Spoon lemon filling into middle of baby Bundt cakes until it flows over the side of the cake. Garnish with organic lemon slices.

Yield: 9 BABY BUNDT CAKES

marilyn and strawberries

A sugar-free, gluten-free Bundt cake made with whipped cream and organic strawberries.

CAKE

2½ cups all-purpose gluten-free flour

¾ cup potato starch

¾ cup tapioca starch

3 teaspoons Stevia Plus Powder

2 teaspoons gluten-free baking powder

1 teaspoon baking soda

2 teaspoons xanthan gum

½ teaspoon salt

3 large omega-3 eggs

¼ cup grapeseed oil

3 tablespoons water

¾ cup Swerve

¾ cup unsweetened vanilla almond, rice, or soy milk

1 tablespoon vanilla extract

3 droppers Liquid Stevia Vanilla Crème

3 tablespoons strawberry powder

1 cup sliced strawberries

1 tablespoon light agave

FROSTING

1 cup heavy cream

2 tablespoons light agave

1 tablespoon strawberry powder

2 cups strawberries, sliced and fanned, for decorating

Note: Strawberry powder can be ordered from Wilderness Family Naturals at 866-936-6457. You can also substitute fresh cranberry juice for pink color.

For Cake: Preheat oven to 350 degrees. Spray-oil a 12-cup Bundt pan and flour with gluten-free flour; set aside.

Sift together gluten-free flour, potato starch, tapioca starch, Stevia Plus Powder, baking powder, baking soda, xanthan gum, and salt; set aside. In stand-up mixer using wire attachment, beat eggs, oil, and water on high until frothy, about 5 minutes. Lower speed and mix in Swerve, milk, vanilla, liquid stevia, and strawberry powder.

In stand-up mixer, change to a paddle attachment on low and add dry ingredients to wet ingredients. Beat as little as possible. In small bowl, toss sliced strawberries in agave and fold strawberries gently into batter.

Pour batter into prepared cake pan. Let sit for 5 minutes. Bake for 35–40 minutes or until an inserted toothpick comes out clean. Cool and transfer to wire rack before frosting.

For Frosting: Chill mixing bowl in freezer for 20 minutes. Beat chilled heavy cream, agave, and strawberry powder until cream forms soft peaks. Frost cake while frosting is fresh and cold. Top with sliced strawberries. Keep cake refrigerated.

Yield: 1 **BUNDT CAKE**

voluptuous volcano cakes

Individual chocolate cakes that ooze a fudge-like chocolate filling.

¾ cup butter or vegetable butter

1½ cups grain-sweetened chocolate chips (See gluten-free note)

3 large organic omega-3 egg yolks

3 large organic omega-3 eggs

½ cup Swerve

3 tablespoons light agave

1 tablespoon vanilla

3 droppers Liquid Stevia Chocolate

½ cup plus 1 tablespoon all-purpose gluten-free flour

¼ cup tapioca starch

⅓ cup unsweetened dark cocoa powder, plus extra for dusting

....

Gluten-Free Note: Grain-sweetened chocolate chips may contain malted barley, which contains gluten. For a gluten-free substitute, over medium heat in a double boiler, melt 2 ounces unsweetened baking chocolate in a double boilers over medium heat. Stir in an extra ¼ cup Swerve or ZSweet and substitute this mixture for melted grain-sweetened chips. Then stir in remaining ingredients.

Preheat oven to 350 degrees. Butter 6 ramekins (6 ounces each) and dust with dark cocoa powder. Tap out excess cocoa, but make sure ramekins are well coated; set aside.

In double boiler, melt butter and chocolate chips. Set aside to cool slightly.

In stand-up mixer with paddle attachment, beat eggs, egg yolks, Swerve, agave, vanilla, and liquid stevia on medium-high speed for about 5 minutes until mixture is thick and light yellow in color. Add in the melted chocolate mixture and blend on low speed.

In small bowl, sift together gluten-free flour, tapioca starch, and cocoa powder. Gradually add dry mixture to wet mixture and blend.

Pour the batter into prepared ramekins, filling them to ⅛ inch from the top. Place on baking tray and bake for exactly 13 minutes. Check that oven temperature is correct. The cake is done when toothpick inserted into center comes out clean. Remove from the oven and cool for 3 minutes. Run a paring knife between the cake and ramekin to loosen. Invert your dessert plate over the ramekin (be careful, they're hot) and flip over. Tap the plate lightly and lift off the ramekin. Garnish with raspberries.

Yield: **6 INDIVIDUAL CAKES**

mocha maca crumb cake

A sweet espresso-chocolate flavored coffee cake.

1½ cups yacon powder

½ cup dark agave

½ cup vanilla lactose-free whey or rice protein powder

2 teaspoons cinnamon

2 teaspoons Stevia Plus Powder

3 droppers Liquid Stevia Cinnamon

3 droppers Liquid Stevia Chocolate

¾ cup butter or vegetable butter

¾ cup vegetable shortening

1 cup low-fat buttermilk or unsweetened soy milk

1 omega-3 egg

3 tablespoons roasted maca

1 teaspoon baking soda

1 teaspoon gluten-free baking powder

1 teaspoon xanthan gum

1 teaspoon nutmeg

½ teaspoon salt

Preheat oven to 350 degrees. Spray-oil an 8x8-inch baking dish or pan and flour with gluten-free flour; set aside.

In medium bowl, mix yacon powder, agave, protein powder, cinnamon, Stevia Plus Powder, and liquid stevias.

Cut in vegetable butter and vegetable shortening with two forks or a pastry cutter until dough forms little balls the size of peas. Take out 1 cup of this mixture for topping; set aside.

Transfer rest of batter to stand-up mixer and with a paddle attachment mix in buttermilk and egg. Beat a few times on low. In another separate bowl, mix together roasted maca, baking soda, baking powder, xanthan gum, nutmeg, and salt. Add dry ingredients to wet mixture and beat on low. Be careful to not overbeat.

Pour batter into prepared baking dish. Spread topping that was set aside earlier evenly on top of batter. Use a foil tent over top of whole baking dish to protect topping from browning too quickly. Bake for 30–35 minutes or a toothpick inserted into the middle comes out clean. Cool in pan on wire rack.

Yield: **16 SERVINGS**

blueberry poundless cake

A blueberry and lemon Bundt cake with sugar-free lemon glaze.

CAKE

1 cup plus 1 tablespoon all-purpose gluten-free flour

1 cup sweet sorghum flour

½ cup potato starch

¼ cup tapioca starch

1½ teaspoons gluten-free baking powder

½ teaspoon baking soda

2 teaspoons xanthan gum

¼ teaspoon salt

1 teaspoon cinnamon

1 cup vegetable butter

1¾ cups Swerve

4 omega-3 eggs

1 tablespoon lemon zest

2 tablespoons lemon juice

2 tablespoons vanilla extract

1 cup unsweetened almond milk

1½ cups blueberries

GLAZE

1½ cups confectioners' Swerve

2 tablespoons lemon juice

2 tablespoons light agave

lemon zest, for garnish

For Cake: Preheat oven to 350 degrees. In medium bowl, sift together gluten-free flour, sorghum flour, potato starch, tapioca starch, baking powder, baking soda, xanthan gum, salt, and cinnamon; set aside.

In stand-up mixer with paddle attachment, cream butter until smooth. Add in Swerve and beat until frothy, about 2 minutes. Beat in eggs one at a time. Add lemon zest, lemon juice, and vanilla. With paddle attachment in stand-up mixer, slowly beat dry mixture into wet mixture starting with flour and alternating with almond milk. Fold in blueberries dredged in remaining 1 tablespoon gluten-free flour with spatula.

For best baking results, spoon batter into a 12-cup silicone ungreased Bundt pan. If you use a metal Bundt pan, grease and flour the pan before spooning in batter. Spray-oil a butter knife and carefully run the knife through the batter to eliminate air holes. Bake for 45–50 minutes, or until knife tip inserted into the middle comes out clean. Cool completely on wire rack.

For Glaze: In small bowl, whisk together confectioners' Swerve, lemon juice, and agave. Drizzle glaze on cooled cake. Garnish with lemon zest.

Yield: 1 BUNDT CAKE

pineapple carrot cake

A fruity carrot cake with cream cheese frosting.

1½ cups all-purpose gluten-free flour

½ cup tapioca starch

1 teaspoon baking soda

1¼ teaspoons gluten-free baking powder

1 teaspoon xanthan gum

2 teaspoons cinnamon

2 large omega-3 eggs

½ cup grapeseed oil

¾ cup Swerve

¼ cup agave

¼ cup carrot juice

2 droppers Liquid Stevia Cinnamon

1½ cups finely shredded carrot

¾ cup crushed, unsweetened pineapple, with juice

1 recipe for Cream Cheese Frosting

For Cake: Preheat oven to 350 degrees. Spray-oil two 8x8-inch cake pans and dust with gluten-free flour; set aside.

Sift together gluten-free flour, tapioca starch, baking soda, baking powder, xanthan gum, and cinnamon; set aside.

In stand-up mixer with wire-whisk attachment, beat the eggs and oil on high until frothy, about 5 minutes. Mix in Swerve, agave, carrot juice, and liquid stevia. Mix in shredded carrot and pineapple. Change to paddle attachment and slowly add in dry mixture to wet mixture. Be careful to not overmix batter.

Pour batter into prepared baking pans. Use a spray-oiled spatula to scrape out all batter. Bake cakes for 30–35 minutes or until golden brown. Check cakes halfway through and if browning too quickly, cover with foil tents. Cakes are done when a wooden toothpick inserted into the middle comes out clean. Cool on wire rack.

For Frosting: Make 2 recipes for Cream Cheese Frosting. Place first cake on a cake plate and frost the top leaving the sides bare. Place second cake on top and frost just the top layer.

Yield: ONE CAKE

cream cheese frosting

A sugar-free cream cheese frosting.

2 3-ounce packages cream cheese

½ cup butter, vegetable butter,
or Earth Balance 50/50

2 teaspoons vanilla

½ cup agave

1½ cups confectioners' Swerve

In stand-up mixer, beat cream cheese, vegetable butter, vanilla, and agave. Run confectioners' Swerve through a sifter. Gradually add powdered and sifted Swerve to cream cheese mixture and beat well.

Yield: ABOUT 2½–3 CUPS

vegan cream cheese frosting

A healthy sugar-free, dairy-free nut frosting.

1 cup raw almonds, unsalted

1 cup raw cashews, unsalted

3 cups filtered water

½ cup agave

½ cup unsweetened almond milk

2 teaspoons vanilla

1½ cups confectioners' Swerve

Place almonds, cashews, and water in medium bowl and cover. Let nuts soak overnight in refrigerator. Drain and rinse nuts thoroughly and pat dry with paper towel. To food processor, add soaked nuts, agave, almond milk, and vanilla. Purée until well blended.

Run confectioners' Swerve through a sifter. Gradually add sifted Swerve to nut mixture in food processor through spout while continuing to blend. For a thinner frosting, transfer frosting to high-powered blender and blend on low to high adding a bit more unsweetened almond milk. Scrape out frosting with spatula.

Yield: ABOUT 2½-3 CUPS

vanilla babycake cupcakes

A vanilla cupcake with vanilla frosting.

CUPCAKES

¾ cup all-purpose gluten-free flour

¾ cup white rice flour

½ cup tapioca starch

¼ cup potato starch

1 teaspoon baking soda

2 teaspoons gluten-free baking powder

1 teaspoon xanthan gum

½ teaspoon nutmeg

¼ teaspoon fine sea salt

2 large omega-3 eggs

½ cup grapeseed oil

1 cup Swerve

½ cup light agave

½ cup unsweetened almond milk

2 teaspoons vanilla extract

2 droppers Liquid Stevia Vanilla Crème

FROSTING

1½ cups confectioners' Swerve

2 tablespoons butter or vegetable shortening

2 tablespoons unsweetened almond milk, unsweetened soy milk, or water

1 dropper Liquid Stevia Vanilla Crème

2 teaspoons light agave

For Cupcakes: Preheat oven to 350 degrees. Line cupcake trays with silicone baking cups or foil liners; set aside.

Sift together gluten-free flour, white rice flour, tapioca starch, potato starch, baking soda, baking powder, xanthan gum, nutmeg, and salt; set aside.

In stand-up mixer with wire-whisk attachment, beat the eggs and oil until frothy, about 5 minutes. Add in Swerve, agave, almond milk, vanilla, and liquid stevia and mix well. Change to paddle attachment and slowly add dry mixture to wet mixture. Be careful to not overmix batter.

Spoon batter into prepared cupcake trays to three-quarters of the way full. Bake in the center of the oven for about 20–25 minutes, until firm. At 15 minutes, check to see if cupcakes are browning too quickly, and if so, cover with foil tent. Cupcakes are done when a wooden toothpick inserted into the middle comes out clean. Briefly cool on a wire rack. Remove cupcakes from baking tin and continue to cool in liners for 30 minutes. Remove cupcakes from liners and place on serving dish.

For Frosting: In stand-up mixer with paddle attachment, cream together confectioners' Swerve and butter. Add in milk or water, liquid stevia, and agave. Frost cooled cupcakes.

Yield: **12 CUPCAKES**

chocolate babycake cupcakes

A dark chocolate cupcake with chocolate frosting.

CUPCAKES

¾ cup all-purpose gluten-free flour

¾ cup white rice flour

½ cup tapioca starch

¼ cup cocoa powder

1 teaspoon baking soda

2 teaspoons gluten-free baking powder

1 teaspoon xanthan gum

¼ teaspoon fine sea salt

2 large omega-3 eggs

½ cup grapeseed oil

1 cup Swerve

½ cup agave

½ cup unsweetened almond milk

2 teaspoons vanilla extract

3 droppers Liquid Stevia Chocolate

FROSTING

1½ cups confectioners' Swerve

2 tablespoons butter or vegetable shortening

2 tablespoons almond milk, unsweetened soy milk, or water

1 dropper Liquid Stevia Chocolate

2 teaspoons agave

2 tablespoons unsweetened cocoa powder

For Cupcakes: Preheat oven to 350 degrees. Line cupcake trays with silicone baking cups or foil liners; set aside.

Sift together the gluten-free flour, white rice flour, tapioca starch, cocoa powder, baking soda, baking powder, xanthan gum, and salt; set aside.

In stand-up mixer with wire-whisk attachment, beat the eggs and oil on high until frothy, about 5 minutes. Add in Swerve, agave, almond milk, vanilla, and liquid stevia and mix well. Change to paddle attachment and slowly add in prepared dry mixture to wet mixture. Be careful to not overmix batter.

Spoon batter into prepared cupcake trays to three-quarters of the way full. Bake in center of oven for about 20–25 minutes, until firm. At 15 minutes, check to see if cupcakes are browning too quickly, and if so, cover with a foil tent. Cupcakes are done when a wooden toothpick inserted into the middle comes out clean. Briefly cool on a wire rack. Remove cupcakes from tray and continue to cool in liners for 30 minutes. Remove cupcakes from liners and place on serving dish.

For Frosting: In stand-up mixer with paddle attachment, cream together confectioners' Swerve and butter. Add in milk or water, liquid stevia, and agave. Blend in cocoa powder until smooth. Frost cooled cupcakes.

Yield: **12 CUPCAKES**

pies, tarts, and crisps

Of all the sugar-free and gluten-free recipes and techniques I have discovered and developed, I am most happy and excited about the piecrust. This recipe has only recently been perfected since its debut on *The Sweet Truth* on Veria TV when I made Kelly's Pumpkin Pie and Gran's Strawberry-Rhubarb Pie. The upgrades I have made to the piecrust recipe include chilling all the ingredients and using ice water. I replaced vegetable shortening with Earth Balance Natural Shortening sticks or 50/50 sticks. Both products are refrigerated and help maintain the durability of the piecrust, and allow it to be flaky. When I taught this recipe using the Earth Balance shortening sticks, my baking students loved the results and were amazed at the flaky texture and buttery taste. Using cold butter is usually the best choice for taste for most people, so I recommend butter as an ingredient in gluten-free piecrust recipes. Instead of cutting in the chilled fat with a pastry cutter or forks, I now use the food processor to easily and quickly mix the dough.

Using these methods, you will make a foolproof piecrust that acts and looks like a wheat piecrust. You will be able to roll out the dough to your desired thickness and to flip it over into the pie plate without breaking the crust. You'll be able to trim the edges of the crust with kitchen shears without having the crust break off the edges of the pie plate. You will also be able to fold the piecrust under and crimp the edges to your own desired design with ease. Swiftness is the key to making crust. This ensures that you are keeping the ingredients cold. Make the crust on a work surface away from the heat of the oven so the ingredients have the best chance of remaining chilled.

Other baking tools include: a glass pie plate, wax paper, a pastry mat, a rolling-pin sleeve, a foil tent, and egg washes or baths. A glass pie plate is preferred over metal or tin because the glass will conduct heat properly for best baking results. Using a sleeve generously dusted with gluten-free flour on your rolling pin ensures the crust won't stick to your rolling pin. A pastry mat under two sheets of wax paper will secure your work surface to roll out piecrust evenly. Dust the wax paper lightly with gluten-free flour. And foil tents protect the gluten-free crust from browning too quickly. Finally, an egg bath applied with a silicone pastry brush creates a golden finish on the edges of the pie and protects the crust from burning.

The recipe for this traditional, flaky piecrust is found in Very Berry Blue Pie and Pecan Pie. If you are new to sugar-free and gluten-free baking and pie making, start with Open-Face Apple Crumble Pie, which uses a crust that is made in the food processor with gluten-free oats and almonds and is pressed into the bottom of a glass pie plate and chilled to make firm.

Note that it is possible that people with celiac disease may not tolerate gluten-free oats. A great gluten-free pie alternative is the raw, vegan Yin-Yang Cheesecake. You will dehydrate this crust in the dehydrator and use soaked nuts for the cream filling.

OPEN-FACE APPLE CRUMBLE PIE

PECAN PIE

VERY BERRY BLUE PIE

GRAN'S STRAWBERRY-RHUBARB PIE

KELLY'S PUMPKIN PIE

CHOCOLATE CHIP PIZZA

YIN-YANG CHEESECAKE

PEACEFUL PEAR AND POMEGRANATE TART

PASSIONATE PEACH CRISP

open-face apple-crumble pie

An apple-crumble pie with a crust made with gluten-free oats.

CRUST

1½ cups gluten-free rolled oats

½ cup coconut-date rolls

1 tablespoon all-purpose
gluten-free flour

3 tablespoons Swerve or ZSweet

¼ teaspoon fine salt

¼ cup butter or Earth Balance
Natural Shortening sticks

2 tablespoons agave

2 tablespoons ice water

FILLING

3½ pounds Fuji and
Granny Smith apples

2 tablespoons lemon juice

⅓ cup Swerve or ZSweet

¾ teaspoon cinnamon

¼ teaspoon nutmeg

2 tablespoons unsalted butter
or vegetable butter

CRUMBLE

¾ cup all-purpose
gluten-free flour

¾ cup almond meal

¼ cup Swerve or ZSweet

¼ cup unsalted butter
or vegetable butter

For Crust: In food processor, place rolled oats, coconut-date rolls, gluten-free flour, Swerve or ZSweet, and salt. Blend until finely ground. Cut shortening into small pieces and add to oat mixture in food processor. Pulse about 5–6 times until combined and then blend for 20–30 seconds.

Add agave and ice water. Pulse until just combined. Batter will be crumbly. Evenly and firmly, press the prepared crust mixture into the bottom, up the sides, and onto the rim of a 9-inch glass pie plate. Press the edges firmly. Freeze pie shell for 15 minutes. Preheat oven to 350 degrees.

For Filling: Peel, core, and cut apples into ¼-inch-thick slices. In large bowl, toss together the apples, lemon juice, Swerve or ZSweet, cinnamon, and nutmeg. Pour mixture into prepared pie shell, mounding apples more toward the center. Cut butter into small pieces and dot on top of pie filling.

For Crumble: In small bowl, combine flour, almond meal, and Swerve or ZSweet. With pastry cutter or two forks, cut in butter until mixture resembles coarse crumbs. Use fingers to squeeze mixture together into pea-size pieces. Sprinkle the crumb topping over the apples to cover completely. Bake pie for about 1 hour. Cool on wire rack.

Yield: 1 PIE

pecan pie

A traditional pecan pie made with a flaky gluten-free crust.

CRUST

1 cup all-purpose
gluten-free flour

½ cup potato starch

¼ cup arrowroot

1 teaspoon xanthan gum

1 teaspoon Stevia Plus Powder

1 cup butter or Earth Balance
All Natural Shortening sticks

2 large omega-3 eggs

2 tablespoons ice cold water

1 tablespoon cold vinegar

Note: Chill all the above piecrust ingredients overnight and use cold. Make piecrust swiftly and away from heat. This will ensure your gluten-free dough will roll out easily, won't tear, and will bake correctly. For rolling the crust, use wax paper on top of a pastry mat or pastry cloth and a generously floured sleeve on your rolling pin. A glass pie plate is best for baking.

For Crust: Preheat oven to 400 degrees. Prepare work surface with a pastry mat or pastry cloth covered in two sheets of wax paper. Lightly flour top surface of wax paper and flour the sleeve that covers the rolling pin.

Sift together gluten-free flour, potato starch, arrowroot, xanthan gum, and Stevia Plus Powder. Pour dry ingredients into food processor. With sharp knife, cut butter or shortening into 5–6 tablespoons and then cut those pieces in half and add to flour mixture. Pulse butter and flour together until mixture looks like small crumbs the size of peas; set aside. In small bowl, whisk together one egg, water, and vinegar. Add this wet mixture to food processor and pulse 3–4 times. The mixture will form into a ball of dough.

Scoop out dough with hands, form into a ball, and place dough on prepared work surface between sheets of wax paper. Roll out dough for a 9-inch pie plate (about 13 inches in diameter). Try not to overwork dough. Flip rolled out piecrust into glass pie plate. With pastry shears, trim edges of piecrust so that 1 inch hangs over edge. Gently fold the trimmed edge of piecrust under, all around the pie. Crimp edges of piecrust to your desired design (a simple fluted border works best). Beat remaining egg and moisten edges of piecrust with pastry brush. Fill piecrust up with pie weights or dried beans (about 2 pounds) and bake for 8 minutes at 400 degrees. When done, remove beads or weights and cool crust on wire rack.

FILLING

3 large omega-3 eggs

2 tablespoons unsweetened almond milk

½ cup dark agave

¾ cup Swerve

¼ cup coconut sugar or yacon syrup

4 tablespoons butter or vegetable butter, melted

1 tablespoon vanilla extract

2 droppers Liquid Stevia Vanilla Crème

⅔ cup pecans, coarsely chopped

12 pecan halves

For Filling: In medium bowl, whisk together eggs, almond milk, agave, Swerve, coconut sugar or yacon syrup, melted butter, vanilla, and liquid stevia. Add chopped pecans.

Pour filling into cooled pie shell. Arrange 12 pecan pieces around pie in a circle. Cover pie with a foil tent. Reduce oven heat to 350 degrees and bake for 45–50 minutes. Cool on wire rack.

Yield: 1 **PIE**

very berry blue pie

A blueberry pie with cinnamon and nutmeg.

CRUST
(enough for one crust)

1 cup all-purpose gluten-free flour

½ cup potato starch

¼ cup arrowroot

1 teaspoon xanthan gum

1 teaspoon Stevia Plus Powder

1 cup butter or Earth Balance All Natural Shortening sticks

1 organic omega-3 egg

2 tablespoons ice cold water

1 tablespoon cold vinegar

1 egg, beaten

Note: Chill all the above piecrust ingredients overnight and use cold. Make piecrust swiftly and away from heat. This will ensure your gluten-free dough will roll out easily, won't tear, and will bake correctly. For rolling the crust, use wax paper on top of a pastry mat or pastry cloth and a generously floured sleeve on your rolling pin. A glass pie plate is best for baking.

For One Crust (you will need two): Prepare work surface with a pastry mat or pastry cloth covered in two sheets of wax paper. Lightly flour surface of wax paper and flour the rolling-pin sleeve.

Sift together gluten-free flour, potato starch, arrowroot, xanthan gum, and Stevia Plus Powder. Pour dry ingredients into food processor. With sharp knife, cut butter or shortening stick 5–6 tablespoons and then cut those pieces in half and add to flour mixture. Pulse butter and flour together until mixture looks like small crumbs the size of peas; set aside. In small bowl, whisk together egg, water, and vinegar. Add this wet mixture to food processor and pulse 3–4 times until dough forms into a ball of dough.

Scoop out dough with hands, form into a firm ball, and place dough on prepared work surface between sheets of wax paper. Roll out dough for a 9-inch pie plate (about 13 inches in diameter). Try not to overwork dough. Flip rolled out piecrust on top of glass pie plate. Brush the rim of prepared bottom pie shell with an egg bath. Repeat piecrust recipe for top; set top crust aside.

FILLING

8 cups fresh blueberries

½ cup Swerve

¼ cup cornstarch

1 tablespoon fresh lemon juice

¼ teaspoon cinnamon

¼ teaspoon nutmeg

2 tablespoons unsalted butter or vegetable butter

1 large omega-3 egg

For Filling: Preheat oven to 400 degrees. Place blueberries in a large bowl. With your hands, crush about ½ cup of berries, letting them fall back into the bowl. Add the Swerve, cornstarch, lemon juice, cinnamon, and nutmeg and stir. Spoon mixture into bottom pie crust, mounding berries toward the center. Cut butter into small pieces. Dot pie filling with butter.

Place the second piece of dough on top of blueberries. Gently press the top and bottom piece of dough together to seal. With pastry shears, trim edges of piecrust so that 1 inch hangs over edge all around. Tuck dough under and crimp edge as desired. In a small bowl, beat egg and brush over entire surface of the pie with an egg bath. Sprinkle extra Swerve over top of crust.

Place pie on a parchment-lined baking sheet. Bake pie at 400 degrees for 20 minutes. Cover pie with foil tent. Reduce oven temperature to 350 degrees and bake for another 40–45 minutes. Cool completely on wire rack.

Yield: 1 **PIE**

gran's strawberry-rhubarb pie

A strawberry-rhubarb custard pie in a protein-packed, gluten-free, flakey vanilla crust.

CRUST
(enough for one crust)

1½ cups all-purpose gluten-free flour

½ cup potato starch

½ cup arrowroot

½ cup lactose-free vanilla whey protein powder

1 teaspoon xanthan gum

⅛ teaspoon gluten-free baking powder

2 teaspoons Stevia Plus Powder

1 cup butter or Earth Balance All Natural Shortening sticks

1 organic omega-3 egg

2 tablespoons water

1 tablespoon apple cider vinegar

1 egg yolk

1 tablespoon water

Note: Chill all the above piecrust ingredients overnight and use cold. Make piecrust swiftly and away from heat. This will ensure your gluten-free dough will roll out easily, won't tear, and will bake correctly. For rolling the crust, use wax paper on top of a pastry mat or pastry cloth and a generously floured sleeve on your rolling pin. A glass pie plate is best for baking.

For One Crust (you will need two): Prepare work surface with a pastry mat or pastry cloth covered in two sheets of wax paper. Lightly flour top surface of wax paper and flour the sleeve that covers the rolling pin.

Sift together gluten-free flour, potato starch, arrowroot, protein powder, xanthan gum, baking powder, and Stevia Plus Powder. Cut in shortening with two forks or pastry cutter until mixture looks like small crumbs the size of peas.

In small bowl, whisk together egg, water, and vinegar. Add this to prepared mixture, mix well, and use hands to form into a ball.

Place dough on prepared work surface between sheets of wax paper. Carefully roll out crust until it is big enough to fit in a 9-inch pie plate (around 13 inches in diameter). Carefully, but quickly, remove top sheet of wax paper and flip crust into pie plate. Flute edges. If the crust breaks, this is normal. Press it back together. You will have plenty of crust leftover for patching.

In a small cup, beat egg yolk and water. With pastry brush, coat fluted edges with an egg yolk bath.

FILLING

4 tablespoons unsweetened almond milk

2 teaspoons kuzu

3 large omega-3 eggs, beaten

½ cup yacon powder

½ cup plus 2 tablespoons light agave

⅓ cup lactose-free vanilla whey protein powder or vanilla rice protein powder

3 tablespoons strawberry powder or all-fruit jam (See note)

2 droppers Stevia Liquid Lemon Drops

1 teaspoon nutmeg

2 tablespoons all-purpose gluten-free flour

2 cups chopped rhubarb

2 cups sliced strawberries

1 tablespoon lemon juice

2 tablespoons vegetable butter

Note: Strawberry powder can be ordered from Wilderness Family Naturals at 866-936-6457. You can also substitute all-fruit strawberry jam.

For Filling: Preheat oven to 400 degrees. In stand-up mixer with paddle attachment, beat almond milk and kuzu together until kuzu is dissolved. Add 3 beaten eggs and mix. Add yacon, ½ cup agave, protein powder, strawberry powder, liquid stevia, nutmeg, and gluten-free flour. Beat until smooth. In medium bowl, toss chopped rhubarb and sliced strawberries in remaining agave and lemon juice. Place fruit mixture into prepared piecrust.

Pour custard mixture over fruit. Cut up vegetable butter and dot over fruit and custard filling. Place second crust on top. Flute edges. Once pie is assembled, give it an egg yolk bath. Cover pie with a foil tent.

Bake for 50–60 minutes or until crust is golden brown and firm. Best to let pie cool and then place in fridge for an hour in order for custard to set.

Yield: 1 PIE

kelly's pumpkin pie

CRUST

1 cup all-purpose
gluten-free flour

½ cup potato starch

¼ cup arrowroot

1 teaspoon xanthan gum

1 teaspoon Stevia Plus Powder

1 cup butter or Earth Balance
All Natural Shortening sticks

2 large omega-3 eggs

2 tablespoons ice-cold water

1 tablespoon cold vinegar

Note: Chill all the above piecrust ingredients overnight and use cold. Make piecrust swiftly and away from heat. This will ensure your gluten-free dough will roll out easily, won't tear, and will bake correctly. For rolling the crust, use wax paper on top of a pastry mat or pastry cloth and a generously floured sleeve on your rolling pin. A glass pie plate is best for baking.

For Crust: Preheat oven to 400 degrees. Prepare work surface with a pastry mat or pastry cloth covered in two sheets of wax paper. Lightly flour top surface of wax paper and flour the sleeve that covers the rolling pin.

Sift together gluten-free flour, potato starch, arrowroot, xanthan gum, and Stevia Plus Powder. Pour dry ingredients into food processor. With sharp knife, cut butter or shortening into 5–6 tablespoons and then cut those pieces in half and add to flour mixture. Pulse butter and flour together until mixture looks like small crumbs the size of peas; set aside. In small bowl, whisk together 1 egg, water, and vinegar. Add this wet mixture to food processor and pulse 3–4 times. The flour mixture will form into a ball of dough.

Scoop out dough with hands, form into a ball, and place dough on prepared work surface between sheets of wax paper. Roll out dough for a 9-inch pie plate (around 13 inches in diameter). Try not to overwork dough. Flip rolled out piecrust into glass pie plate. With pastry shears, trim edges of piecrust so that 1 inch hangs over edge. Gently fold the trimmed edge of piecrust under, all around the pie. Crimp edges of piecrust to your desired design (a simple fluted border works best). Beat remaining egg and moisten edges of piecrust with pastry brush. Fill piecrust up with pie weights or dried beans (about 2 pounds) and bake for 8 minutes at 400 degrees. When done, remove beads or weights and cool crust on wire rack.

FILLING

2 large omega-3 eggs

1 can (15 ounces) unsweetened pumpkin

½ cup light agave

¼ cup Swerve

2 droppers Liquid Stevia Vanilla Crème

2 teaspoons cinnamon

2 teaspoons pumpkin pie spice

½ teaspoon ground ginger

½ teaspoon nutmeg

½ teaspoon allspice

2 tablespoons vanilla extract

2 rounded tablespoons cashew butter

1 tablespoon all-purpose gluten-free flour

Note: To use fresh pumpkin, roast a 2-pound whole pumpkin at 400 degrees for about 50–60 minutes or until a knife easily clears the flesh. Let cool. Cut out a circular hole at the top, remove vine, and cut pumpkin in half. Remove seeds and skin and measure 2 cups for recipe. Freeze the rest of the pumpkin.

For Filling: In stand-up mixer, beat eggs and then add pumpkin, agave, Swerve, liquid stevia, cinnamon, pumpkin pie spice, ginger, nutmeg, allspice, vanilla, cashew butter, and gluten-free flour. Mix well. Pour into prebaked piecrust.

Cover pie with a foil tent. Continue baking pie at 400 degrees for another 12 minutes. Reduce oven to 350 degrees and bake for 40 minutes.

Yield: 1 **PIE**

chocolate chip pizza

Pizza can be made sugar-free and gluten-free and can also be made as a sweet. This decadent dessert is a sweet twist on a classic gluten-free dough with a ricotta topping. I have included recipes for a sweet dessert crust and a traditional crust. Use either and add your own sweet or savory toppings.

SWEET CRUST

3 tablespoons golden flaxseeds

¾ cup all-purpose gluten-free flour

1 cup tapioca flour

¼ cup maca powder

⅓ cup whey protein powder or rice protein powder

1½ teaspoons xanthan gum

½ teaspoon salt

½ cup hot water

1 tablespoon active dry yeast

1 teaspoon light agave

½ teaspoon Stevia Plus Powder

¼ cup warm water

3 tablespoons grapeseed oil

1 teaspoon apple cider vinegar

2 large egg whites, at room temperature

grapeseed oil to grease pizza

Note: Using agave to activate yeast may not produce any fizzing. To ensure activation of the yeast, 1 teaspoon of sugar may be used instead of agave.

Place flaxseeds in a coffee grinder and blend for a few seconds until finely ground. Line pizza pan with parchment paper and sprinkle with ground flaxseeds; set aside.

In stand-up mixer, combine gluten-free flour, tapioca, maca, whey or protein powder, xanthan gum, and salt; set aside.

In separate small bowl, combine hot water, yeast, agave, and Stevia Plus Powder. Let stand until it fizzes; set aside.

In another separate small bowl, combine warm water, 2 tablespoons grapeseed oil, and vinegar. Whisk together and add oil mixture to flour mixture. Blend well. Add in egg whites and blend.

Add wet yeast mixture to stand-up mixer and blend on high speed for 3 minutes. Scrape down sides. Beat on high one more minute. Oil hands with grapeseed oil and scoop out dough. The pizza dough will be very sticky. Form pizza dough into a ball and place on top of greased pan.

Pour remaining tablespoon grapeseed oil on pizza dough. Lightly oil your palms and press out dough into desired shape and thickness (thin is best with gluten-free crust). Shape the edges to hold pizza toppings. Let dough rise 20 minutes in a warm place. You can place dough on the stovetop of a preheated oven covered with plastic wrap and a clean dish towel draped on top of dough.

Top with favorite toppings or chocolate ricotta topping (page 142).

TRADITIONAL CRUST

3 tablespoons
golden flaxseeds

¾ cup all-purpose
gluten-free flour

½ cup tapioca flour

½ cup white rice flour

½ cup potato starch

1½ teaspoons xanthan gum

½ teaspoon salt

2 large egg whites,
at room temperature

¼ cup warm water

2 teaspoons apple cider vinegar

2 tablespoons grapeseed oil

½ cup hot water

1 tablespoon plus 2 teaspoons
active dry yeast

1 tablespoon light agave

Note: Using agave to activate yeast may not produce any fizzing. To ensure activation of the yeast, 1 teaspoon of sugar may be used instead of agave.

Preheat oven to 375 degrees. Place flaxseeds in a coffee grinder and blend for a few seconds. Spread ground flaxseeds on parchment-lined baking sheet large enough for a pizza; set aside.

In medium bowl, sift together gluten-free flour, tapioca starch, white rice flour, potato starch, xanthan gum, and salt; set aside.

In stand-up mixer with wire-whisk attachment, beat egg whites until white and fluffy, about 3–4 minutes. Continue beating and add warm water, vinegar, and oil.

In small bowl, combine hot water, yeast, and agave. Let stand until it fizzes; set aside.

In stand-up mixer, change to paddle attachment on slow speed and add dry ingredients to egg-white mixture. Dough will form small crumbs the size of peas. Mix in the yeast mixture and beat on high for 3 minutes.

Spray-oil a spatula and scrape down sides of bowl, forming dough into a ball. With spray-oiled spatula, turn out dough onto prepared baking sheet and flatten out to desired thickness (thin is best for a gluten-free pizza). With spray-oiled fingers, shape edge around the pizza to hold toppings. Cover with spray-oiled plastic wrap.

Let dough rise 45 minutes in a warm place. You can place dough on the stovetop of a preheated oven covered with plastic wrap and a clean dish towel draped on top of dough. When crust has risen, bake crust alone for 7 minutes. Remove crust from oven and spread desired toppings on top of prebaked crust. Bake another 15 minutes or until crust is golden brown. Cool on wire rack. This will keep the gluten-free dough from becoming soggy.

TOPPING

1½ cups low-fat ricotta

⅓ cup light agave

1 tablespoon vanilla extract

1 dropper Liquid Stevia
Chocolate

1 dropper Liquid Stevia
Vanilla Crème

⅓ cup unsweetened carob chips
(See note)

Preheat oven to 375 degrees. In mixing bowl, blend ricotta, agave, vanilla, and liquid stevias. Don't overmix. Fold in carob chips. Spoon ricotta mixture onto sweet crust (or prebaked traditional crust if using) and spread evenly. Bake for 20 minutes. Remove pizza from pan and cool on wire rack. This will keep the gluten-free dough from becoming soggy.

Note: Instead of carob chips, you may use ⅓ cup grain-sweetened chocolate chips. However, grain-sweetened chocolate chips may contain malted barley, which contains gluten. For a gluten-free substitute use ⅓ cup raw cacao nibs.

yin-yang cheesecake

 It's about balance: a gluten-free, raw, vegan cheesecake made with agave, almonds, and cashews.

CRUST

1 cup coconut-date rolls or
1½ cups chopped Medjool dates

¾ cup dry Brazil nuts

¼ cup almond meal

1 teaspoon cinnamon

dash of water or almond milk,
if needed

FILLING

1 cup raw organic almonds, soaked

1 cup raw organic cashews, soaked

4 tablespoons light agave

1 tablespoon vanilla extract

3 droppers Liquid Stevia
Vanilla Crème

½ cup plus 2 tablespoons
unsweetened almond milk

1 tablespoon lemon juice

1 teaspoon cinnamon

½ cup unsweetened
organic coconut

3 droppers Liquid Stevia
Chocolate

3 rounded tablespoons
roasted carob powder

Note: Add more almond milk for thinner batter, if necessary. To make batter superfine, blend 1 cup at a time in a high-powered blender.

For Crust: Spray-oil a 9-inch glass pie plate; set aside. In food processor with S blade, blend coconut-date rolls, Brazil nuts, almond meal, and cinnamon until it forms a ball. Add water or almond milk one teaspoon at a time if needed for wetness. Remove S blade from food processor and transfer crust to pie plate. Press down into the center of pie plate with thumb and then palm, and flatten and shape dough into a piecrust. Place crust in dehydrator at 105 degrees for 6 hours. Remove from dehydrator and allow to cool.

For Filling: In food processor, blend almonds, cashews, agave, vanilla, Liquid Stevia Vanilla Crème, almond milk, lemon juice, cinnamon, and coconut until smooth. Separate batter evenly into two medium bowls.

To one bowl of batter add Liquid Stevia Chocolate and carob until well mixed. You should now have a vanilla batter and a chocolate batter. Next, assemble pie into yin-yang shape.

For Assembly: Cut out a 4x9-inch piece of cardboard and cut into a S shape. Cover neaty with foil. Spray-oil both sides of the foiled cardboard and place in the middle of the prepared dehydrated piecrust. Now spread the vanilla filling. Keep the S-shape foil-covered cardboard in place and spread the carob/chocolate filling. Gently remove foil-covered cardboard and you should see a perfect yin-yang shape.

Allow cheesecake to chill in refrigerator at least 2 hours before serving.

Yield: 1 **PIE**

peaceful pear and pomegranate tart

A rustic roasted pear and pomegranate tart with pistachio crust.

CRUST

¾ cup butter or Earth Balance All Natural Shortening sticks

¾ cup Swerve

2 large omega-3 egg yolks

1¼ cups all-purpose gluten-free flour

1 teaspoon xanthan gum

⅛ teaspoon gluten-free baking powder

½ teaspoon salt

½ cup unsalted roasted and shelled pistachios

2 teaspoons heavy cream

For Crust: Spray-oil an 11-inch tart pan with removable base; set aside.

In stand-up mixer with paddle attachment, cream the butter first, then add Swerve and beat on low speed until combined, about 2 minutes. Add egg yolks and mix until well combined.

In small bowl, sift together gluten-free flour, xanthan gum, baking powder, and salt. With paddle attachment, add dry mixture to butter mixture and blend until smooth.

Grind pistachios in coffee grinder or high-powered blender to a medium-fine flour. Measure ½ cup ground pistachios and add to stand-up mixer with paddle attachment and mix on low. Add cream and continue to blend. Dough will be soft but will not stick to fingers. Chill dough in refrigerator for at least 30 minutes. After 30 minutes, remove dough from refrigerator. Preheat oven to 350 degrees.

Spray-oil two large spoons and drop dough evenly around prepared tart pan. Place a sheet of spray-oiled plastic wrap over dough in tart pan and press down with a 10-inch cake pan to flatten. Remove cake pan and with flat edge of measuring cup spread dough evenly to edges of tart pan. Carefully remove plastic wrap and press dough into tiny fluted edges around tart pan. Only go to the edge of the top of the tart pan and not over it to ensure the crust doesn't break off.

Line the shell with a piece of parchment paper slightly larger than the pan. Place 10-inch cake pan in lined tart shell and bake until edges are just beginning to turn golden brown, about 15 minutes. Remove cake pan and parchment paper. Continue to bake for another 10 minutes or until crust is golden all over and looks dry. Transfer to wire rack to cool completely. After about 20 minutes, remove tart shell from pan and place on serving platter.

FILLING

6 firm, ripe Bosc pears

½ cup plus 2 tablespoons dark agave

2 tablespoons butter or vegetable butter

½ cup heavy cream, very cold

3 tablespoons light agave

1 cup mascarpone cheese

½ cup coconut cream butter, melted and cooled

½ teaspoon cinnamon

½ cup pomegranate seeds

Note: Unsweetened Coconut Cream Butter can be found under the brands Let's Do…Organic and Aritsana.

For Filling: Cut two unpeeled pears in quarters lengthwise, leaving one quarter of each pear with stem intact. Cut remaining pears in quarters lengthwise and remove the stems. Core all pears and remove inner fibers; set aside.

In a large, heavy sauté pan over medium heat, melt vegetable butter and dark agave. Reserve a quarter of each ingredient if all pears do not fit into sauté pan (you may have to do two rounds of pear sauté).

Heat butter and agave, stirring with wooden spoon until it just begins to bubble. Carefully place pear quarters cut side down in agave/butter and cook, turning occasionally, until a knife goes through flesh with ease, about 10–12 minutes. If mixture starts to smoke, reduce heat to low or carefully remove from heat while pan cools. Pears should be tender and golden amber colored. Carefully remove pears from pan and place on baking sheet to cool completely.

In stand-up mixer, beat very cold heavy cream with light agave until soft peaks form. In separate bowl, gently stir mascarpone cheese with spatula until creamy, then gently fold into whipped cream so as to not overmix. With paddle attachment, beat in coconut cream and cinnamon until just combined. Do not overbeat. (If coconut cream is solid, the temperature in your kitchen is below 76 degrees. If so, measure coconut cream and melt in a small saucepan over low heat, cool completely, and then add to cheese mixture.)

Immediately assemble tart. Dot prepared cheese mixture evenly into tart crust and spread with spatula. Add sliced pears lengthwise into clockwise fan shape around the edges of the tart. Make smaller inner circle with the pears fanning in the same direction. The two pears with stems should be placed in the middle. Sprinkle with pomegranate seeds, drizzle with remaining dark agave, and refrigerate until served.

Yield: **1 TART**

passionate peach crisp

A baked peach dessert made with organic peaches, cinnamon, nutmeg, and agave and topped with a sugar-free crumble.

2½ pounds fresh peaches, peeled, pitted, and sliced

½ cup plus 2 tablespoons light agave

1 teaspoon vanilla extract

2 teaspoons cinnamon

1 teaspoon nutmeg

½ cup all-purpose gluten-free flour

3 tablespoons Swerve

½ cup gluten-free rolled oats or dried mulberries

½ cup butter or vegetable butter, softened

½ cup chopped pecans

....

Note: This recipe can be made with apples, pears, mangoes, or a combination of these fruits with an added ½ cup of berries of your choice.

Preheat oven to 375 degrees. Butter an 8x8-inch square baking dish; set aside.

In large mixing bowl, toss sliced peaches with agave, vanilla, cinnamon, and nutmeg. Place sliced peaches into the prepared baking dish.

Sift together the gluten-free flour and Swerve into a medium bowl. In mini-food processor, add raw oats or dried mulberries and pulse 10 times to grind coarsely. Add oats or mulberries to flour mixture and stir. Cut vegetable butter into flour mixture with pastry cutter or two forks until mixture resembles a coarse meal.

Sprinkle crumble evenly over peaches in baking dish. Sprinkle pecans over crumble. Drizzle remaining 2 tablespoons of agave over pecan and crumbles. Cover baking dish with a foil tent.

Bake for 30 minutes, remove foil tent, and continue to bake for another 15–20 minutes or until crumble is golden and peaches are bubbling.

Yield: **9 SERVINGS**

puddings and kantens

Kantens are low-calorie desserts that are free of white sugar, refined flour, and dairy and are popular among the macrobiotic community. They look and taste like a gelatin mold but are completely vegan. Kantens are made with seasonal fruit and fruit juice. The kanten recipes in this cookbook were created to satisfy my top cravings so I could eat them daily. Four Apples Dessert tastes like an apple pie in fall weather. Toot for Tarts Lemon Squares call to my endless taste for sweet lemon anything. And Think Pink Think Thin is made with pink grapefruit and naturally pink kanten colored with strawberry powder or fresh cranberry juice. I especially love the concept of Think Pink Think Thin because the Japanese use agar agar flakes desserts to slim down and stay trim.

To make these light, delicious treats you will need to use agar agar flakes as a replacement for gelatin. Another main ingredient that you will use is kuzu. Kuzu has a distinct texture and taste that many people in the macrobiotic community know and admire, for kuzu soothes the intestines and helps aid in digestion. Kuzu is easily used to thicken fruit purées, soups, stews, sauces, and raw, vegan desserts. Love Dove Carob Pudding is a low-calorie pudding made dairy-free, sugar-free, and gluten-free with kuzu. Always use kuzu diluted in cold liquid before stirring into the recipe you want to thicken. This way, the kuzu will never clump.

FOUR APPLES DESSERT

TOOT FOR TARTS LEMON SQUARES

PEAR AND TAHINI CREAM CHEESE PIE

LOVE DOVE CAROB PUDDING

THINK PINK THINK THIN

POWER PUDDING

four apples dessert

A spiced apple kanten with raisins that tastes like apple pie filling and is very low in calories.

4 Fuji apples

2 cups apple juice or cider

2 cups filtered water

4 tablespoons agar agar flakes

¼ cup raisins

½ teaspoon cinnamon

2 tablespoons lemon juice

2 droppers Liquid Stevia Vanilla Crème

2 tablespoons light agave

Wash and cut apples into bite-size chunks. You may peel them or leave the skin on. Place in medium mixing bowl. Pour lemon juice over apples and toss; set aside.

In medium saucepan, add apple juice, water, and agar agar flakes. Stirring constantly over medium heat, bring to just under a boil until agar agar flakes is dissolved and then reduce to a simmer.

Add cut apples and lemon juice, raisins, cinnamon, liquid stevia, and agave to saucean. Simmer about 15 minutes or until apples are cooked al dente.

Pour mixture into an 8x8-inch glass baking dish. Cool for 10 minutes and then let set in the refrigerator for at least 2 hours.

Yield: **9 SERVINGS**

toot for tarts lemon squares

 A sweet, tangy kanten made with almonds and lemons that tastes like lemon square filling.

¼ cup lemon juice

1¾ cups unsweetened almond milk

3 tablespoons Swerve or ZSweet

2 tablespoons light agave

4 tablespoons agar agar flakes

¼ cup sliced almonds

sliced almonds and lemon slices, for garnish

In medium saucepan over medium heat, add almond milk and lemon juice. Stirring constantly, whisk in Swerve or ZSweet and agave. Bring to a simmer and stir in agar agar flakes. Stir constantly until agar agar flakes is dissolved, about 5 minutes.

Grind almonds in high-powered blender. Stir ground almonds into sauce pan. Pour lemon and almond mixture into an 8x8-inch glass dish and let cool a few minutes.

Place in the refrigerator to set for at least 2 hours. For best results, chill overnight. When sufficiently chilled, the kanten will be very firm. Cut into squares and serve with extra sliced almonds and lemon slices.

Yield: 16 SQUARES

pear and tahini cream cheese pie

A dairy-free pie with a cream-cheese flavor in a kanten crust made with raw tahini and agave.

CRUST

4 tablespoons agar agar flakes

1 cup water

1 cup apple cider

½ cup raw almond butter or walnut butter

1½ cups raw tahini, unsalted

3 droppers Liquid Stevia Vanilla Crème

2 tablespoons dark agave

2 teaspoons cinnamon

1 tablespoon vanilla extract

TOPPING

3 ripe Bartlett or Bosc pears

½ cup apple cider

1 tablespoon lemon juice

2 tablespoons light agave

2 tablespoons Swerve

1 teaspoon pumpkin pie spice

2 tablespoons kuzu

2 tablespoons water

½ cup raw walnuts, chopped

For Crust: In medium saucepan over medium heat, dissolve agar agar flakes in water and cider by bringing liquids to a boil and then lowering heat to a simmer. Whisk in almond butter, then tahini. Stir in stevia, agave, cinnamon, and vanilla. Pour mixture into an 8x8-inch glass baking dish and chill for at least 1 hour.

For Topping: Peel and slice pears and place in food processor with apple cider, lemon juice, agave, Swerve, and pumpkin pie spice. Blend until smooth. Place pear mixture in medium saucepan over medium flame. In small cup, mix kuzu and water until kuzu is dissolved and add to pear mixture, stirring constantly for about 10 minutes or until thick like a pudding. Pour over chilled tahini pie bottom and chill for another hour. Sprinkle chopped walnuts on top.

Yield: 9 **SERVINGS**

love dove carob pudding

A satisfying carob pudding that tastes like chocolate and is made with kuzu to soothe the stomach and strengthen the intestines.

1 cup plus 2 tablespoons unsweetened almond milk

1 cup water

2 droppers Liquid Stevia Chocolate

2 droppers Liquid Stevia Vanilla Crème

2 tablespoons agave

½ cup carob powder

2 tablespoons kuzu

1 teaspoon chopped Brazil nuts, sliced almonds, or flaked coconut, for garnish

In medium saucepan over medium heat, bring 1 cup almond milk, water, liquid stevias, and agave to a simmer. Whisk in carob powder one tablespoon at a time until blended. Cook for 5–7 minutes, stirring constantly.

In small cup, stir kuzu into remaining 2 teaspoons cold almond milk and blend until smooth. Add dissolved kuzu to carob mixture. Stirring constantly, cook carob mixture for another 2–3 minutes. Mixture will thicken into a pudding.

Spoon pudding into custard cups three-quarters of the way full and chill for 2 hours. Cover with plastic wrap. Keep refrigerated. Garnish with a crunchy topping to serve.

Yield: **4 SERVINGS**

think pink think thin

A Japanese dessert made with agar agar flakes, pink grapefruit, and agave.

1 cup unsweetened pink grapefruit juice

2 cups water

4 tablespoons agar agar flakes

2 tablespoons unsweetened cranberry juice

3 tablespoons light agave

1 dropper Liquid Stevia Lemon Drops

2 large organic pink grapefruits, peeled and sectioned

In medium saucepan over medium heat, bring grapefruit juice, water, and agar agar flakes to a boil. Add cranberry juice, agave, and liquid stevia. Cook for 5 minutes until agar agar flakes dissolves; set aside. Place peeled grapefruit sections into an 8x8-inch glass baking dish. Pour agar agar flakes mixture over grapefruit. Let set for at least 2 hours in refrigerator or chill overnight.

Yield: **9 SERVINGS**

power pudding

Dates, Brazil nuts, dark agave, and cinnamon make a great energy "pudding" and female energy elixir.

6 coconut-date rolls

½ cup raw carob

2 tablespoons dark agave

2 droppers Liquid Stevia Chocolate

½ cup unsweetened almond milk

2 teaspoons vanilla extract

2 teaspoons cinnamon

6 Brazil nuts

In food processor, purée coconut-date rolls, carob, agave, liquid stevia, almond milk, vanilla, cinnamon, and Brazil nuts. Spoon into custard cups and store in refrigerator.

Yield: **4 SERVINGS**

ice cream and sorbets

Making sugar-free ice cream is very easy. You will use an ice cream maker as directed and substitute sugar with erythritol. Ice Cream Any Day is a recipe for an ice cream sundae. I made it on my show, *The Sweet Truth*, and the crew could not believe how good it tasted, or should I say how "real" it tasted. Of course, it is made with heavy cream, but by using the alternative sweetener, erythritol, the glycemic index of the recipe is lowered dramatically. This is definitely a special-occasion sweet treat. Way Watermelon Sorbet is made according to manufacturer's directions using an ice cream maker, yet this summertime dessert is light and refreshing with a hint of fresh lime and lemon-flavored liquid stevia.

CAROB ICE CREAM

ICE CREAM ANY DAY

WAY WATERMELON SORBET

carob ice cream

An easy carob ice cream made with frozen bananas and almond milk.

2 ripe bananas, frozen

½ cup plus 2 tablespoons unsweetened almond milk

1 dropper Liquid Stevia Vanilla Crème

1 dropper Liquid Stevia Chocolate

¼ cup roasted carob powder

¼ cup raw almonds

2 tablespoons agave

¼ teaspoon cinnamon

1 tablespoon raw cacao nibs, for topping

Note: If ice cream is too thin, add extra banana or ice; if it's too thick, add extra almond milk.

The night before, peel 2 bananas. Cut each one into fourths and wrap in a sheet of foil. Freeze bananas overnight.

When bananas are frozen, unwrap and place in food processor with liquid stevias, roasted carob, almonds, agave, and cinnamon. Slowly add almond milk through the food processor's spout.

Purée for about one minute until batter is icy, creamy, and smooth like soft-serve ice cream. Top with raw cacao nibs.

Yield: **4 SERVINGS**

ice cream any day

A sugar-free strawberry and banana ice cream with sugar-free fudge topping.

ICE CREAM

1½ cups sliced strawberries

1 ripe banana

1 tablespoon lemon juice

2 cups cold heavy cream

1 cup cold whole milk

½ cup Swerve or ZSweet

2 teaspoons vanilla extract

1 tablespoon cranberry juice
for color (optional)

TOPPING

4 ounces unsweetened
baking chocolate

½ cup light agave

2 tablespoons Swerve or ZSweet

2 tablespoons unsweetened
almond milk

2 teaspoons vanilla extract

For Ice Cream: Chill bowl or canister from ice cream maker at least 6 hours or according to manufacturer's instructions.

In an 11-cup food processor, purée strawberries, banana, and lemon juice. Add cream, milk, Swerve or ZSweet, vanilla, and cranberry juice. Pulse a few times to mix. Put frozen bowl or canister into ice cream machine, turn machine on, and pour mixture from food processor into opening at top of machine one cup at a time. Once mixture is in frozen bowl or cannister in the ice cream maker, let machine run for 25–30 minutes.

For Topping: In double boiler, melt chocolate with agave and Swerve or ZSweet. Whisk in almond milk and vanilla until smooth. Immediately drizzle over frozen ice cream and garnish with freshly sliced strawberries, freshly sliced banana, or Spanish peanuts, if desired.

Yield: **10 SERVINGS**

way watermelon sorbet

A refreshing watermelon sorbet made with a hint of lime.

1 small seedless watermelon

¼ cup filtered water

½ cup Swerve or ZSweet

3 droppers Liquid Stevia Lemon Drops

3 tablespoons organic lime juice

Chill bowl or canister from ice cream maker at least 6 hours or according to manufacturer's instructions.

Trim and cube watermelon and measure 8 cups of cubed fruit. Add to food processor and purée. Measure 4 cups (about 4 pounds) of the purée and place in large mixing bowl. You may have some watermelon and watermelon purée leftover.

In separate small bowl, whisk together water, Swerve or ZSweet, liquid stevia, and lime juice until Swerve or ZSweet is dissolved. Add mixture to watermelon purée and stir until combined. Put frozen bowl or canister into ice cream machine, turn machine on, and pour mixture from food processor into ice cream maker one cup at a time. Once the mixture is in the frozen bowl or canister, let machine run for 25–30 minutes. Serve with fresh raspberries and kiwi. Store in the freezer.

Yield: **6 SERVINGS**

candy

Candy is my favorite chapter in this cookbook because when I first went sugar-free and gluten-free, it was the one food I could not live without, and I took extra-special care to make the candy that makes me the happiest. This section may become your favorite and most visited selection of recipes because it holds Hemp Ball Truffles and Peanut Butter Cups. To me, and to every one of my friends, my family, and my cooking-class students, these two chocolate candies are absolute winners. That means even your husband or your dad or your kids will like them. Hemp Ball Truffles are omega-3 chocolate candies made with a full vegan protein source from hemp butter. Peanut Butter Cups are made with extra-virgin coconut oil, and from what I have heard from everyone who has tasted them, they are better than the peanut butter cups I ate as a kid (you know the ones).

In the Peanut Butter Cup recipe, use organic Valencia peanut butter that has no added palm oil or cane juice. In both the Hemp Balls and Peanut Butter Cups, I use raw cacao powder and nibs, hempseeds, Liquid Stevia Chocolate, Liquid Stevia Vanilla Crème, and/or Liquid Stevia Cinnamon. These recipes call for any of the three stevias, but you can use just one liquid stevia flavor or all three by mixing and matching. For the candy recipes, liquid stevia is used with agave for a rounded sweet taste and also to spike the flavor. If you want to eliminate the stevia, that is okay. It is used for extra sweetness, not volume or moisture. I don't recommend eliminating the agave because in the candy recipes, it is used for sweetness, moisture, and binding.

For an alternative to chocolate, Berry Balls are truffles using tahini and carob. The recipe also uses dried mulberries for an alternative to raisins. Spanish Peanut Popcorn Balls is an old recipe from my great-grandmother's cookbook that I transcribed using agave instead of corn syrup. And as a gluten-free note, Kashi Haystacks use grain-sweetened chocolate chips, which contain malted barley, which contains gluten. For a substitute, I suggest melting an unsweetened cocoa bar and mixing in Swerve. Swerve has the best tasting sweetness for chocolate candy especially when blended with agave and liquid stevia. Most of the candy recipes use only agave and liquid stevia. The candy recipes are a great way to start setting up your sugar-free and gluten-free pantry because you'll want to make these recipes many times over for the entire family.

fudge it

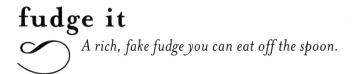

A rich, fake fudge you can eat off the spoon.

2 teaspoons agave

1 rounded tablespoon raw tahini

2 rounded tablespoons carob powder

1 teaspoon vanilla extract

½ teaspoon cinnamon

1 dropper Liquid Stevia Chocolate

1 tablespoon unsweetened almond milk

Blend all ingredients in glass bowl with a spoon. Scoop out and eat off a spoon, or form into a ball and roll in coconut or hempseeds.

Yield: **ABOUT ½ CUP**

almond joy cups

A sugar-free, Almond Joy—type candy made with coconut oil, carob, almonds, and agave.

1½ cups extra-virgin coconut oil, melted

¼ cup organic raw almond butter

3 droppers Liquid Stevia Vanilla Crème

3 droppers Liquid Stevia Chocolate

4 tablespoons agave

1 tablespoon vanilla extract

2 teaspoons cinnamon

¾ cup roasted carob powder

¼ cup hempseeds

¼ cup almond meal

¼ cup unsweetened coconut

Line mini-cupcake trays with paper liners; set aside.

In small sauce pan, melt coconut oil over low heat.

In medium bowl, place melted coconut oil and almond butter. Stir until blended. Whisk in liquid stevias, agave, and vanilla. Add cinnamon and stir until it is evenly blended. Slowly stir in carob a tablespoon at a time. The mixture should still be slightly runny. Add almond meal, hempseeds, and coconut. When combined, the mixture will run off the spoon very slowly.

Spoon into prepared mini-cupcake trays. Pour in mixture to halfway full. Chill in freezer for 15 minutes. When the candies are set, pop out and store in a freezer-safe container. Keep frozen.

Yield: **50 CANDIES**

hemp ball truffles

 A sweet, raw, vegan carob truffle made with hemp butter and agave and rolled in hempseeds.

½ cup raw hemp butter

4 tablespoons agave

2 droppers Liquid Stevia Chocolate

4 tablespoons hemp milk

1 teaspoon cinnamon

1 tablespoon vanilla extract

2 rounded tablespoons roasted carob powder

4 rounded tablespoons raw cacao powder

1 tablespoon raw cacao nibs

1 tablespoon goji berries

3 tablespoons hempseeds

In small bowl, blend hemp butter, agave, liquid stevia, hemp milk, cinnamon, and vanilla. With flat spatula fold in carob and cacao by alternating a tablespoon of each at a time until batter is smooth, pliable, and shiny like fudge. Fold in cacao nibs and goji berries.

Roll into 1-inch balls and roll in hempseeds.

Yield: 15 **TRUFFLES**

kashi haystacks

Crunchy chocolate desserts made with toasted buckwheat groats, carob chips, and agave.

¼ cup grain-sweetened
chocolate chips
(See gluten-free note)

¼ cup unsweetened carob chips

1 tablespoon extra-virgin
coconut oil

2 droppers Liquid Stevia
Vanilla Crème

2 tablespoons dark agave

1 teaspoon vanilla

1 teaspoon cinnamon

1 cup toasted buckwheat groats

....

Note: For extra crunch, add 2 rounded tablespoons ground raw cacao nibs and 2 tablespoons goji berries after you add in the toasted buckwheat groats.

....

Gluten-Free Note: Grain-sweetened chocolate chips may contain malted barley, which contains gluten. For a gluten-free substitute, melt 1 ounce unsweetened baking chocolate in a double boiler over medium heat. Stir in an extra 3 tablespoons Swerve or ZSweet and substitute this mixture for melted grain-sweetened chips.

Line two mini-cupcake trays with paper liners; set aside.

In double boiler over medium heat, melt chocolate chips, carob chips, coconut oil, liquid stevia, agave, and vanilla.

When mixture is melted, stir in cinnamon and toasted buckwheat groats until they are completely coated. Remove double boiler from heat.

Spoon a tablespoon of the mixture into lined mini-baking tins. Each haystack will take on its own shape when spoon-dropped into the cups. Place in freezer for 10 minutes. Store in refrigerator.

Yield: 12 HAYSTACKS

peanut butter cups

A sugar-free organic chocolate peanut butter cup made with agave.

CANDY

1½ cups extra-virgin
coconut oil, melted

¾ cup roasted peanut butter

1 tablespoon organic vanilla extract

2 teaspoons cinnamon

3 droppers Liquid Stevia
Vanilla Crème

3 droppers Liquid Stevia
Chocolate

4 tablespoons light agave

¾ cup roasted carob powder

½ cup raw cacao powder

½ cup raw cacao nibs

½ cup hempseeds

FILLING

1 cup roasted peanut butter

4 tablespoons agave

For Candy: Line mini-cupcake tins with paper liners; set aside.

Melt coconut oil by placing jar under hot water or spoon into saucepan and melt over low flame. When coconut oil turns to a liquid, pour oil in medium bowl. Slowly whisk in peanut butter until smooth.

Whisk in vanilla, cinnamon, liquid stevias, and agave one at a time. Slowly stir in carob powder and cocoa powder a spoonful at a time. Stir raw cacao nibs and then stir in hempseeds. Batter should run off of spoon easily, but should not be too runny.

For Filling: In separate bowl, mix peanut butter and agave with a spatula until smooth.

Spoon ½ teaspoon of the peanut butter filling into prepared cupcake trays. Spoon prepared chocolate/carob batter on top of peanut butter mixture three-quarters of the way to top of cupcake liner. Chill in freezer for 15 minutes. Store in the freezer.

Yield: **50 CANDIES**

mint-chocolate patties

A sugar-free, organic mint chocolate with a hint of hemp.

1½ cups extra-virgin coconut oil, melted

¾ cup hemp butter

½ cup confectioners' Swerve

1 teaspoon peppermint extract

3 droppers Liquid Stevia Peppermint Drops

3 droppers Liquid Stevia Chocolate

¼ cup agave

¾ cup roasted carob powder

½ cup raw cacao powder

½ cup raw cacao nibs

½ cup hempseeds

Line mini-cupcake tray with paper liners; set aside.

Melt coconut oil by placing jar under hot water or spoon into saucepan and melt over low flame. When coconut oil turns to a liquid, pour oil in medium bowl. Slowly whisk in hemp butter until smooth, then whisk in confectioners' Swerve. Add in peppermint extract, liquid stevias, and agave one at a time and blend.

Slowly stir in carob powder and cocoa powder a spoonful at a time. Stir in raw cacao nibs and then stir in hempseeds. Batter should run off of spoon easily, but should not be too runny. Spoon batter into prepared mini-cupcake tins. Chill in freezer for 15 minutes. Store in freezer.

Yield: **50 CANDIES**

berry ball truffles

A simple, non-chocolate truffle with goji berries and mulberries.

½ cup raw tahini

4 tablespoons agave or yacon syrup

2 droppers Liquid Stevia Cinnamon

4 tablespoons unsweetened almond milk

1 tablespoon vanilla extract

1 teaspoon cinnamon

6 rounded tablespoons raw carob powder

2 tablespoons mulberries

2 tablespoons goji berries

3 tablespoons unsweetened shredded coconut, plus extra for rolling

In small bowl, blend tahini, agave, liquid stevia, almond milk, vanilla, and cinnamon. With flat spatula, fold in carob powder a tablespoon at a time until the batter is smooth, pliable, and shiny like fudge. With spatula, fold in goji berries, mulberries, and coconut. Form into 1-inch balls and roll in coconut.

Yield: 25 BALLS

spanish peanut popcorn balls

A sugar-free popcorn snack made with agave and Spanish peanuts.

1 cup light agave

2 tablespoons butter
or vegetable butter

½ cup Swerve

1 tablespoon kuzu

1 tablespoon cold water

2 teaspoons apple cider vinegar

15 cups freshly popped popcorn

1 cup Spanish peanuts

Line two baking sheets with wax paper; set aside.

Over medium-low heat in a medium saucepan, heat agave, butter, and Swerve until thick like a syrup (just about to a boil, about 5 minutes). In small cup, dissolve kuzu in water and vinegar. Add to saucepan. Stir constantly until thick and reduce liquid for another 15 minutes. Remove from heat. Let cool for 5 minutes.

Place popcorn and peanuts in 8-quart sauce pan. Pour wet ingredients from saucepan over popcorn and peanuts and stir with a long wooden spoon until evenly coated. Let sit another 5–10 minutes to cool, otherwise the popcorn will fall apart because it will still be too warm to stick together.

Spray-oil a 1-cup dry measuring cup so popcorn won't stick and scoop out a big scoop of popcorn mixture. Flip cup over and place popcorn mixture onto prepared baking sheet. Lightly spray-oil fingers and mold popcorn into a tight ball with the bottom staying flat on the wax paper.

Repeat with remaining popcorn mixture. Refrigerate popcorn balls for at least one hour to set. Keep refrigerated.

Yield: 9 OVERSIZED BALLS

cherry bombs

 A raw, vegan dessert truffle made with cherries, Brazil nuts, and coconut cream.

⅓ cup unsweetened coconut cream butter

½ cup roasted carob powder

1 tablespoon raw cacao powder

2 tablespoons dark agave

2 droppers Liquid Stevia Chocolate

2 droppers Liquid Stevia Dark Chocolate

1 cup fresh cherries, pitted and halved

1½ cups Brazil nuts

½ cup unsweetened carob chips (See dairy-free note)

Note: Unsweetened Coconut Cream Butter can be found under the brand Let's Do...Organic and Artisana.

Dairy-Free Note: Carob chips may contain whey from dairy, so for a substitute, use ½ cup raw cacao nibs.

Line two mini-cupcake trays with paper liners; set aside.

In food processor, purée coconut cream butter, carob, cocoa powder, agave, liquid stevias, cherries, and Brazil nuts. When batter is formed, gently pulse in carob chips. With a tablespoon, scoop out batter, form into balls, and place in prepared cupcake trays. Freeze for 15 minutes (tops of cherries will get frostbite if kept in the freezer any longer) and serve. Keep refrigerated.

Yield: **30 TRUFFLES**

hearts in dark chocolate

Pineapple and strawberries dipped in sugar-free dark chocolate sauce.

16 ounces strawberries, cleaned, with stem on

1 large pineapple, cut into ¼-inch round slices

2 ounces unsweetened baking chocolate

3 tablespoons light agave

2 droppers Liquid Stevia Chocolate

1 teaspoon vanilla extract

2 tablespoons Swerve

2 rounded tablespoons unsweetened coconut cream butter

¼ teaspoon cinnamon

3 tablespoons unsweetened almond milk

Note: Unsweetened Coconut Cream Butter can be found under the brands Let's Do...Organic and Artisana.

For Fruit: Wash and dry strawberries. Keep stems on and place in a bowl; set aside. Cut and trim a fresh pineapple into ¼-inch round slices; set aside. Line a baking sheet with parchment paper; set aside.

For Dipping Sauce: Over medium flame in a double boiler, melt unsweetened chocolate, agave, liquid stevia, vanilla, Swerve, and coconut cream butter. Mix until smooth. Whisk in cinnamon, then whisk in almond milk. Mix chocolate sauce again until smooth.

Keep saucepan on stove and turn down flame to low. Dip pineapple slices and strawberries halfway into the dark chocolate sauce and place on the wax paper. You may have leftover fruit and may have to make another round of sauce.

Immediately place in the freezer and let set for at least 10 minutes before serving. Keep refrigerated.

Yield: 12 **SERVINGS**

30-second snacks

With no cooking involved, the recipes in this chapter are great for kids, teens, and folks on the go. The ingredients include many superfoods that are nutrient and calorie dense. Very few servings are needed for a quick pick-me-up. These snacks can be made in less than 30 seconds and are formulated to sustain your energy over several hours. The superfoods you will familiarize yourself with are almond meal, goji berries, raw cacao nibs, and hempseeds.

Almond meal is made of finely ground almonds and provides a good source of polyunsaturated fat. Goji berries are from China and contain high amounts of vitamin C, A, and E, plus trace minerals and amino acids. Raw cacao nibs are raw chocolate pieces without the extra added sugar found in candy bars. They contain many antioxidants and polyphenols. Hempseeds are a full vegan protein source, contain vitamin E, and have a balance of the essential fatty acids omega-3, -6, and -9.

APPLESAUCE AND ALMOND CRUMBLE

TRAIL MIX

LOW-CARB VANILLA YOGURT

SPOON MACAROON

applesauce and almond crumble

A quick mock apple pie with almond and cinnamon crumble.

¾ cup unsweetened applesauce

1 tablespoon almond meal

¼ teaspoon cinnamon

1 teaspoon light agave

Spoon applesauce into custard cup. In small measuring cup mix almond meal, cinnamon, and agave together to make a crumble. Spoon on top of applesauce.

Yield: 1 SERVING

trail mix

 Made with goji berries and raw cacao, this is like dark chocolate and raspberries.

1 rounded tablespoon goji berries

1 rounded tablespoon raw cacao nibs

1 rounded tablespoon unsweetened carob chips

In custard cup, mix goji berries, cacao nibs, and carob chips together. Eat like trail mix.

Yield: 1 SERVING

low-carb vanilla yogurt

Vanilla yogurt sweetened with agave and stevia.

1 cup plain nonfat yogurt

2 teaspoons light agave

½ dropper Liquid Stevia Vanilla Crème

In small bowl, blend yogurt, agave, and liquid stevia.

Yield: 1 **SERVING**

spoon macaroon

A coconut-and-hemp cookie on a spoon.

2 tablespoons hempseeds

1 tablespoon unsweetened coconut

2 teaspoons light agave

⅛ teaspoon cinnamon

In custard cup, mix hempseeds, coconut, agave, and cinnamon. Eat off a spoon.

Yield: 1 **SERVING**

baby food

Even though this is the last chapter, I think it holds the most important recipes. From all my work in the field of public speaking and in leading cooking classes on living a sugar-free and gluten-free lifestyle, it's clear to me that this cookbook is not only for people who want to be more healthy, satisfy their sweet tooth, and eliminate processed sugar and gluten. It also helps families who have children with food allergies focus on cooking and nutrition. It is my priority to help babies grow strong, be balanced, and eat healthfully.

Starting with Cael's Cookies: Blueberry Babies I go back to the basics. I developed this allergy-free, vegan, protein-packed dehydrator cookie for my nephew, Caelan Keough. He is a one-and-a-half year old tot with four teeth and needs help growing. Since I live in California and he lives in New Hampshire, I can only make healthy treats for him that are free of sugar, flour, eggs, and butter and send them off priority mail.

I began the formula for this cookie with the intention of boosting Cael's immune system. I wanted to use a natural fruit with the highest antioxidants and chose the acai berry, which has omega-3 essential fatty acids. Acai is a purple berry and makes a purple cookie, so I added frozen blueberries as a base. This makes for easy blending in the food processor. I also added unsweetened dried blueberries for more color, natural sweetness, and texture. The cookie would not be complete without a full vegan protein source, so hemp butter, hemp protein powder, and hempseed were my best choices.

The cookie has a purply-blue hue that hides the green color of the hemp and spinach. Yes, spinach! I made it the first time without spinach, but the cookie tastes better with it, plus spinach is great for extra iron. I also added a sprouted blend of chia, rice, and flaxseed to give the cookie more protein, an easily digested fiber, and more essential fatty acids. This sprouted blend, made by Navitas Naturals, also acts as a replacement for flour. Cael likes the cookies. It's a start. His six-month-old baby brother, Kellen Keough, is already envious of him. But when Kellen is old enough, I am sure there will be a cookie named after him, too.

The recipes in this chapter are not just for babies, but for adults as well. Little People Pumpkin Pie is a pumpkin pie without the crust. Mango Mama Baby Cereal can be devoured by mother and child at any time of day. Toddler Teething Biscuits are a must-make because there are very few sugar-free and gluten-free baby biscuits that can be store bought. And Baby Mousse Mud is a delicious pudding made with silken tofu, banana, and carob. Indulge!

CAEL'S COOKIES: BLUEBERRY BABIES

LITTLE PEOPLE PUMPKIN PIE

BABY MOUSSE MUD

MANGO MAMA BABY CEREAL

TODDLER TEETHING BISCUITS

cael's cookies: blueberry babies

An allergy-free dehydrator cookie made with immune-boosting acai berries and the vegan protein source of hemp with omega-3.

¼ cup flaxseeds

1 cup frozen blueberries

1 tablespoon lemon juice

2 tablespoons kuzu

1 large handful fresh baby spinach

¼ cup raw hemp butter

¼ cup hemp protein powder, vanilla or plain

¼ cup acai powder

½ cup agave

1 teaspoon alcohol-free vanilla extract

¼ cup hempseeds, plus extra for topping

Place flaxseeds in a coffee grinder and blend until finely ground; set aside.

In food processor, blend frozen blueberries, lemon juice, and kuzu until just combined. Wash and dry spinach. Add spinach to food processor and purée. Add hemp butter, hemp protein powder, ground flaxseeds, acai powder, agave, and vanilla. Purée until well combined. Batter should come together and be thick enough to stand on its own. Pulse in hempseeds until just combined, about 2–3 times.

With 2 spoons, spoon-drop rounded tablespoons full of cookie batter onto Teflex sheets, four across and four down for a total of 16 cookies per sheet. With back of spoon, smooth each cookie mound into a ½-inch high circle. Sprinkle each cookie with extra hempseeds.

Dehydrate cookies at 105 degrees for 28–36 hours, depending whether the soaked flaxseeds are added. If the flaxseeds are added, the cookie will harden faster and less dehydrating is needed. Halfway through, remove cookies from Teflex sheets with thin spatula and transfer to mesh sheets; continue dehydrating.

Yield: **32 COOKIES**

little people pumpkin pie

A mock pumpkin pie filling made with kabocha squash and Fuji apple.

FILLING

1 small kabocha squash

2 tablespoons grapeseed oil

2 organic Fuji apples, rinsed, peeled, and coarsely chopped

2 tablespoons lemon juice

1 teaspoon cinnamon

1 teaspoon nutmeg

1 teaspoon pumpkin pie spice

1 dropper Liquid Stevia Vanilla Crème

3 tablespoons dark agave

½ cup apple cider

1 tablespoon almond milk, if needed

TOPPING (optional)

1 cup heavy cream

1 tablespoon light agave

For Filling: Preheat oven to 400 degrees. Line a baking sheet with parchment paper. Quarter squash, remove seeds and baste with 1 tablespoon oil. Place squash on prepared baking sheet and roast for 15 minutes.

Place chopped apples in a bowl and toss with lemon juice until it covers all the apples. Toss other tablespoon of oil over the apples until the oil is evenly spread.

In small bowl, mix together cinnamon, nutmeg, and pumpkin pie spice. Sprinkle over apples. Add liquid stevia and agave. Toss mixture until apples are covered.

After the squash has roated for 15 minutes, add apple mixture to the baking sheet. Continue to roast for another 15–20 minutes or until apples have caramelized and are fully cooked.

When roasting is done, scoop out squash flesh from skin. Place one cup in food processor and purée with ¼ cup apple cider and ½ cup of roasted apples. Remove mixture into medium bowl. Repeat this process until you have puréed all the squash and apples. Mix together in bowl. If you want to thin it out, add a tablespoon of unsweetened almond milk. Transfer to individual custard cups. Top with a dollop of whipped cream topping, if desired.

For Topping: Chill metal bowl for stand-up mixer in freezer for 2 hours. In stand-up mixer, whip heavy cream with agave until it forms soft peaks.

Yield: **8 SERVINGS**

baby mousse mud

 A carob and protein packed mousse for baby and you.

1 12-ounce package organic firm tofu

½ cup roasted carob powder

1 large ripe banana

2 tablespoons light agave

½ dropper Liquid Stevia Vanilla Crème

¼ teaspoon cinnamon

2 teaspoons arrowroot

ADULT TOPPINGS

3 tablespoons unsweetened carob chips (See dairy-free note)

2 tablespoons sliced almonds

Dairy-Free Note: Carob chips may contain whey from dairy, so for a dairy-free substitute, use ½ cup raw cacao nibs.

In food processor, purée drained tofu, carob, banana, agave, liquid stevia, cinnamon, and arrowroot until smooth. Pour into four 6–8 ounce ramekins. Refrigerate for at least 2 hours before serving. Keep refrigerated.

Serving Suggestion: For adults, mix in unsweetened carob chips and top with sliced almonds.

Yield: **4 SERVINGS**

mango mama baby cereal

A buckwheat baby cereal with mango purée.

2 mangoes, peeled and cubed

2 teaspoons lemon juice

¼ cup buckwheat groats, finely ground

1 cup water

½ cup apple juice

2 tablespoons light agave

ADULT TOPPINGS

extra mango, for garnish

1 tablespoon unsweetened coconut

1 tablespoon slivered almonds

In food processor, purée cubed mangoes and lemon juice; set aside.

To grind buckwheat groats, place in high-powered blender or sturdy coffee grinder. Grind thoroughly. Measure ½ cup of ground groats. You will have some leftover. Put groats through a sifter to extract any pieces that did not grind completely.

In medium saucepan over medium heat, bring ground buckwheat grouts, water, apple juice, and agave to a boil and then simmer for at least 5 minutes, stirring constantly.

When cereal is done and water is absorbed, transfer to a bowl and spoon mango purée on top. Swirl purée through cereal.

Serve with unsweetened milk of choice (almond, rice, soy, or cow).

Serving Suggestion: For adults, add fresh mango chunks, unsweetened coconut, or slivered almonds on top.

Yield: **4 SERVINGS**

toddler teething biscuits

 A soft sugar-free, gluten-free teething cookie sweetened with apple juice and cinnamon.

½ cup golden flaxseeds

1 cup all-purpose gluten-free flour

1 cup brown rice flour

½ cup tapioca starch

½ cup instant nonfat dry milk or rice protein powder

1 teaspoon gluten-free baking powder

1 teaspoon baking soda

1 teaspoon xanthan gum

1 teaspoon cinnamon

½ cup light agave

¼ cup grapeseed oil

1 omega-3 egg

½ cup unsweetened apple juice

Place flaxseeds in coffee grinder and blend until finely ground; set aside.

In medium bowl, sift together gluten-free flour, brown rice flour, tapioca starch, dry milk, baking powder, baking soda, xanthan gum, and cinnamon.

In stand-up mixing bowl with paddle attachment, combine agave and oil. Beat in egg and apple juice. Gradually add dry mixture to wet mixture. Add flaxseeds to dough. Dough will be sticky, but stiff. Dust hands with gluten-free flour and form dough into a ball. Refrigerate for 2 hours.

Preheat oven to 375 degrees. Line baking sheet with parchment paper. Take the parchment paper off baking sheet and place on work surface. Place dough on prepared parchment paper and flatten by placing a bit of gluten-free flour on top of dough and pushing down with palm of hand. Next, place a piece of wax paper on top of dough. Roll dough out to within ½ inch of the edge of parchment. Remove wax paper carefully.

Cut rolled out dough into 2x1-inch bars and place cookies on parchment-paper-lined baking sheet. Bake 15 minutes until light brown. Cool on wire rack.

Yield: **48 BISCUITS**

substitutions

glycemic index and calorie chart

The following chart lists the glycemic index and calories of white table sugar and brown sugar, the two most popular high-glycemic sweeteners used in recipes for baked goods. It compares them to the alternative sugar ingredients used in this cookbook: agave, stevia, eryrthritol, yacon, and coconut or palm sugar.

For example, if you substitute white table sugar with only agave using the standard substitution of ⅔ cup agave for every 1 cup of sugar, the result will yield 80 fewer calories. The recipe will also have a lower GI using only agave. This is because 1 cup of white table sugar has 720 calories and ⅔ cup of agave has only 640 calories. Also, agave is considered a low-glycemic food, with a GI of under 55.

Considering the calorie content and glycemic index of agave, I often use only ½ cup of agave and then blend the agave with stevia and erythritol for the best moisture, sweetness, and volume in a given recipe.

Both stevia and erythritol have a zero glycemic index and zero calories. Blending alternative sweeteners in this way allows for a very sweet product with fewer calories and a lower glycemic index. Most importantly, this method of blending more than one alternative sweetener allows the baked good to taste like it has traditional white sugar or brown sugar.

Note that all product brand names listed are only suggestions. Other brands are available but may have different measuring systems (for example, some brands of liquid stevia do not come with a dropper dispenser and must be measured with a teaspoon).

The glycemic index and calories are approximate:

INGREDIENT	MEASUREMENT	GLYCEMIC INDEX	CALORIES
WHITE TABLE SUGAR	1 TEASPOON	65	15
BROWN SUGAR	1 TEASPOON	65	17
LIQUID STEVIA (Sweet Leaf Liquid Stevia)	¼ TEASPOON	0	0
POWDERED STEVIA (Sweet Leaf Stevia Plus with FOS)	½ TEASPOON	0	0
ERYTHRITOL (ZSweet)	1 TEASPOON	0	0
ERYTHRITOL/OLIGOFRUCTOSE (Swerve)	1 TEASPOON	0	0
ERYTHRITOL/REBIANA (Truvia)	1 TEASPOON	0	0
YACON SYRUP (Navitas Naturals Yacon Syrup)	1 TEASPOON	1	7
AGAVE*	1 TEASPOON	19–35	20
COCONUT SUGAR/PALM SUGAR (Navitas Naturals Palm Sugar and Nature's Blessings Coconut Sugar)	1 TEASPOON	31	15

(1 CUP = 48 TEASPOONS)

*Light or dark, the GI of agave syrup has an approximate range of 19–35 depending on the type of agave plant. Blue weber agave has one of the lowest GIs.

alternative sugar ingredients for baking

The following list includes white table sugar, brown sugar, molasses, honey, and maple syrup and their alternative ingredients, as well as their measurements and substitutions. Not included in this chart are fruits, fruit juices, dried fruits, and raw or roasted carob, which although they are used to sweeten recipes, are not considered alternative, sugar-free ingredients.

There are many brands on the market and online made with erythritol or erythritol and other natural ingredients. I use the brand name Swerve and ZSweet in this cookbook because these are the brands I use in my pantry. You may use other erythritol brands like ZSweet as table sugars. The best-tasting erythritol blend brand for baking is Swerve.

The standard blend of agave, erythritol, and stevia will yield the best taste, moisture, and volume in a given recipe. Also, Truvia, or erythritol/rebiana, should only be used as a table sugar and in measurements of 1 packet per serving in tea, coffee, cereal, etc.

Note that using a straight substitution of 1 cup erythritol (ZSweet) or erythritol/oligofructose (Swerve) for 1 cup of white table sugar will dry out sweets and desserts because these natural alternative sweeteners do not hold moisture in baked goods like white sugar or brown sugar do when blended with butter, eggs, and flour. It is necessary to add a small amount of good fat to a sugar-free, gluten-free recipe.

WHITE TABLE SUGAR

standard substitution for white sugar used for baking:
1 cup sugar = ½ cup light agave, ½ cup Swerve or ZSweet plus 1–2 droppers liquid stevia
(1 dropper = ½ teaspoon)

standard substitution for white sugar used as a table sugar:
1 teaspoon sugar = 1 teaspoon light agave
or
1 teaspoon sugar = 2 teaspoons (one packet) erythritol (ZSweet)
or
1 teaspoon sugar = 2 teaspoons (one packet) erythritol/oligofructose (Swerve)
or
1 teaspoon = 2 teaspoons (1 packet) erythritol/rebiana (Truvia)
or
1 teaspoon sugar = ¼ teaspoon (half dropper) liquid stevia
or
1 teaspoon sugar = ½ teaspoon (1 packet) stevia (Stevia Plus Powder)

BROWN SUGAR

1 cup brown sugar = ½ cup dark agave plus ¼ cup Swerve or ZSweet plus ¼ cup yacon syrup
or
1 cup brown sugar = ½ cup dark agave plus ¼ cup Swerve or ZSweet plus ¼ cup coconut/palm sugar
or
1 cup brown sugar = ½ cup Swerve or ZSweet plus ½ cup yacon syrup or ½ cup coconut/palm sugar or ½ cup dark agave

MOLASSES

1 tablespoon molasses = 1 tablespoon dark agave
or
1 tablespoon molasses = 1 tablespoon yacon syrup

or

1 tablespoon molasses = 1 tablespoon coconut sugar/palm sugar

HONEY

standard substitution for honey:

1 tablespoon honey = 1 tablespoon light agave

MAPLE SYRUP

standard substitution for maple syrup:

1 tablespoon maple syrup = 1 tablespoon dark agave

alternative flour ingredients for baking

The following list is a general recommendation for using gluten-free flours for specific baked goods and their substitutions within the recipes in this cookbook. It can also be used as a guide for transcribing your own personal recipes by switching from gluten flours to gluten-free flours. The list is a guideline that is meant to help you be resourceful in your kitchen. If you are allergic to a certain flour or don't have something on hand in your pantry, you can easily substitute another flour. There are no hard and fast rules for gluten-free flour substitutions.

For the categories of baked goods in the following chart, from brownies to bagels, any of the singly listed flours can be substituted in place of each other. For example, brownies calling for ½ cup of buckwheat flour may be substituted with ½ cup of quinoa flour or ½ cup of brown rice flour, etc. But when you use a mix of all-purpose gluten-free flour, white rice flour, potato flour, potato starch, tapioca starch, and/or arrowroot, only the potato starch, tapioca starch, and arrowroot can be substituted for each other. For example, if you are making a bagel recipe and don't have potato starch handy, you may use tapioca starch in its place, therefore doubling the amount of tapioca starch (using this substitution is also appropriate if you or your child is allergic to potato and you cannot use any potato products).

BROWNIES

½ CUP WHEAT FLOUR = ½ CUP OF ONE OF THE FOLLOWING:

all-purpose gluten-free flour

quinoa flour

a mix of all-purpose gluten-free flour and quinoa flour

a mix of all-purpose gluten-free flour, quinoa flour, and quinoa flakes buckwheat flour

brown rice flour

sorghum flour

a mix of all-purpose flour and gluten-free rolled oats

DROP COOKIES

½ CUP WHEAT FLOUR = ½ CUP OF ONE OF THE FOLLOWING:

- all-purpose gluten-free flour

a mix of all-purpose gluten-free flour and quinoa flour

a mix of all-purpose gluten-free flour, quinoa flour, and quinoa flakes

a mix of all-purpose gluten-free flour and brown rice flour

a mix of all-purpose gluten-free flour and gluten-free rolled oats

CUTOUT COOKIES

½ CUP WHEAT FLOUR = ½ CUP OF ONE OF THE FOLLOWING:

a mix of all-purpose gluten-free flour, white rice flour, potato flour and potato starch, tapioca starch, and/or arrowroot

a mix of all-purpose gluten-free flour, white rice flour, potato flour, baked yam, and potato starch, tapioca starch, and/or arrowroot

PIECRUST

½ CUP WHEAT FLOUR = ½ CUP OF ONE OF THE FOLLOWING:

a mix of all-purpose gluten-free flour, white rice flour, and potato starch, tapioca starch, and/or arrowroot

a mix of all-purpose gluten-free flour, white rice flour, rice or whey protein powder, and potato starch, tapioca starch and/or arrowroot

SWEET BREADS

½ CUP WHEAT FLOUR = ½ CUP OF ONE OF THE FOLLOWING:

all-purpose gluten-free flour

quinoa flour

quinoa flour and flakes

buckwheat flour

brown rice flour

sorghum flour

gluten-free rolled oats

a mix of all-purpose gluten-free flour and buckwheat groats (dry, soaked, or sprouted)

a mix of all-purpose gluten-free flour and baked yam

a mix of all-purpose gluten-free flour and cornmeal or polenta

MUFFINS

½ CUP WHEAT FLOUR = ½ CUP OF ONE OF THE FOLLOWING:

all-purpose gluten-free flour

quinoa flour

quinoa flour and flakes

buckwheat flour

brown rice flour

sorghum flour

a mix of all-purpose gluten-free flour and gluten-free rolled oats

a mix of all-purpose gluten-free flour and buckwheat groats (dry, soaked, or sprouted)

a mix of all-purpose gluten-free flour and baked yam

SCONES

½ CUP WHEAT FLOUR = ½ CUP OF ONE OF THE FOLLOWING:

all-purpose gluten-free flour

quinoa flour

quinoa flour and flakes

buckwheat flour

brown rice flour

sorghum flour

a mix of all-purpose gluten-free flour and gluten-free rolled oats

PANCAKES

½ CUP WHEAT FLOUR = ½ CUP OF ONE OF THE FOLLOWING:

all-purpose gluten-free flour

quinoa flour

quinoa flour and flakes

buckwheat flour

brown rice flour

sorghum flour

gluten-free rolled oats

a mix of all-purpose gluten-free flour and buckwheat groats (dry, soaked, or sprouted)

a mix of all-purpose gluten-free flour and baked yam

a mix of all-purpose gluten-free flour and cornmeal or polenta

WAFFLES

½ CUP WHEAT FLOUR = ½ CUP OF ONE OF THE FOLLOWING:

all-purpose gluten-free flour

quinoa flour

quinoa flour and flakes

buckwheat flour

brown rice flour

sorghum flour

CAKES

½ CUP WHEAT FLOUR = ½ CUP OF THE FOLLOWING:

a mix of all-purpose gluten-free flour, white rice flour, and potato starch, tapioca starch and/or arrowroot

CUPCAKES

½ CUP WHEAT FLOUR = ½ CUP OF THE FOLLOWING:

a mix of all-purpose gluten-free flour, white rice flour, and potato starch, tapioca starch and/or arrowroot

BISCUITS

½ CUP WHEAT FLOUR = ½ CUP OF ONE OF THE FOLLOWING:

all-purpose gluten-free flour

sorghum flour

a mix of all-purpose gluten-free flour and quinoa flour

a mix of all-purpose gluten-free flour and gluten-free rolled oats

YEAST BREADS

½ CUP WHEAT FLOUR = ½ CUP OF ONE OF THE FOLLOWING:

a mix of all-purpose gluten-free flour, white rice flour, and potato starch, tapioca starch and/or arrowroot

a mix of all-purpose gluten-free flour, white rice flour, potato flour, and potato starch, tapioca starch and/or arrowroot with quinoa flour

a mix of all-purpose gluten-free flour, white rice flour, potato flour, and potato starch, tapioca starch and/or arrowroot with gluten-free rolled oats

a mix of all-purpose gluten-free flour, white rice flour, potato flour, buckwheat flour, and potato starch, tapioca starch and/or arrowroot

PIZZA DOUGH

½ CUP WHEAT FLOUR = ½ CUP OF ONE OF THE FOLLOWING:

a mix of all-purpose gluten-free flour, white rice flour, potato starch, potato flour, and tapioca starch and/or arrowroot

a mix of all-purpose gluten-free flour, white rice flour, quinoa flour, potato flour, and potato starch, tapioca starch and/or arrowroot

a mix of all-purpose gluten-free flour, white rice flour, potato flour, polenta or cornmeal, and potato startch, tapioca starch and/or arrowroot

½ CUP WHEAT FLOUR = ½ CUP OF ONE OF THE FOLLOWING:

a mix of all-purpose gluten-free flour, white rice flour, potato flour, and potato starch, tapioca starch, and/or arrowroot

a mix of all-purpose gluten-free flour, white rice flour, gluten-free rolled oats, potato flour, and potato starch, tapioca starch, and/or arrowroot

alternative butter/shortening/oil ingredients for baking

This section lists butter and shortening and their alternative ingredients and substitutions, as well as measurements. In traditional sweet baked-good recipes, the basic four ingredients of butter, sugar, eggs, and flour are the foundation of any batter or dough. The use of butter will always prevail as the best choice in creating a batter or dough with the correct consistency for perfect baking results. This is true whether the butter is softened at room temperature for a drop cookie dough or used cold to make a piecrust. For people who love dairy, it will always be the number one choice for taste, too. But if you want to make a dairy-free dessert or have a dairy intolerance, there are other choices that can substitute for butter and yield good results.

For a dairy-free alternative, butter is best replaced with an all-natural vegetable-oil blend usually consisting of palm oil, olive oil, canola oil, and/or soybean oil. Earth Balance is a brand that makes dairy-free vegetable butters, an all-natural dairy-free shortening, and a 50/50 butter and vegetable oil blend that I use in many recipes.

In the cold-case dairy section of Whole Foods Market or your local health food store, as well as Trader Joe's, Earth Balance can be found as an all-natural buttery spread and comes packed in a tub. This product should be used as a table butter, but can be used in the recipes in this cookbook.

In using dairy-free ingredients for baking recipes where creaming the fat and sugar is called for, the best choice is Earth Balance shortening sticks or 50/50 sticks. The 50/50 sticks come salted or unsalted and are made from half cow butter and half vegetable oil blend using palm oil, olive oil, canola oil, and soybean oil. Both the Earth Balance shortening sticks and 50/50 sticks come in a package with four sticks of butter. Each stick equals ½ cup, just like regular butter does. Both of these products are a great choice for lowering the amount of saturated fat in a recipe. The Earth Balance 50/50 sticks also allow the taste of real butter to be present and are an excellent choice to use for piecrusts.

For shortening kept on your pantry shelf at room temperature, there are several all-natural vegetable shortening products that are made with palm oil. Spectrum All Vegetable Shortening is my first choice followed by Jungle Shortening.

Extra-virgin coconut oil may be used in place of butter in drop cookies, brownies, and sweet breads. If coconut oil is used to replace butter in drop cookies, the prepared cookie dough should be dropped onto prepared baking sheets and placed in the freezer for 30 minutes. Even though the cookie dough made with coconut oil will still spread, freezing the dough will help to prevent the drop cookie dough from spreading too much.

And if you are making a carrot cake or chocolate cake and want to use a healthier choice of oil other than canola, corn, or vegetable oils, substitute with coconut or grapeseed oil.

BUTTER
Earth Balance Shortening sticks
Earth Balance 50/50 sticks, unsalted
Earth Balance Buttery Spread
Organic extra-virgin coconut oil

SHORTENING
Earth Balance Shortening sticks
Earth Balance 50/50 sticks, unsalted
Spectrum Vegetable Shortening
Jungle Shortening

CORN OIL, CANOLA OIL, VEGETABLE OIL
extra-virgin coconut oil
Grapeseed oil

egg replacers

Eliminating eggs in a sugar-free, gluten-free recipe is tricky, but it can be done. Eggs in baked goods give moistness, color, and act as binding and leavening agents. In sugar-free, gluten-free baking, the odds of baked goods sticking together and rising are already slim because the sugar accounts for volume and moistness and the gluten accounts for the leavening agent or ability to allow the ingredients to rise and stick together. Here are vegan substitutes that act as binders and as leavening agents, except in layer or Bundt cakes.

For eggs as binding agents in brownies, cookies, scones, muffins, breakfast breads, coffee cakes, corn bread, and brown bread:

ONE EGG EQUALS ANY OF THE FOLLOWING:

1 tablespoon ground flaxseed in 3 tablespoons water

1 ounce or ¼ cup puréed silken tofu

3 tablespoons puréed fruit or vegetable (applesauce or pumpkin)

1 tablespoon kuzu dissolved in 3 tablespoons cold water

1 tablespoon almond butter, cashew butter, or tahini

1 rounded tablespoon Greek-style yogurt or soy yogurt

½ medium-ripe banana, mashed

(Note: When in doubt, use ground flaxseeds in water or silken tofu.)

For eggs as binding and leavening agents in white breads, bagels, piecrusts, and pizza dough:

ONE EGG EQUALS ANY OF THE FOLLOWING:

1 rounded tablespoon soy flour in 1 tablespoon water

2 tablespoons gluten-free flour, ½ teaspoon grapeseed oil, ½ teaspoon gluten-free baking powder plus 2 tablespoons water

index

recipe index

❦ OTHER ULYSSES PRESS BOOKS

THE 100 BEST VEGAN BAKING RECIPES: COOKIES, CAKES, MUFFINS, PIES, BROWNIES,
AND BREADS TO ROCK YOUR OVEN!
Kris Holechek, $12.95
Baking vegan doesn't mean giving up delicious baked goods. This book offers a wide range
of recipes for naturally healthy and cruelty-free treats that are moist, savory, delicate,
buttery, sweet, and decadent.

THE GI MEDITERRANEAN DIET: THE GLYCEMIC INDEX–BASED LIFE-SAVING DIET
OF THE GREEKS
Dr. Fedon Alexander Lindberg, $14.95
Mediterranean cuisine and GI dieting are a proven match made in culinary heaven. This
book shows readers how the Old World's most celebrated foods can keep you lean,
young, and living a longer and healthier life.

THE JUICE FASTING BIBLE: DISCOVER THE POWER OF AN ALL-JUICE DIET TO
RESTORE GOOD HEALTH, LOSE WEIGHT, AND INCREASE VITALITY
Dr. Sandra Cabot, $12.95
Offering a series of quick and easy juice fasts, this book provides a reader-friendly
approach to an increasingly popular, alternative health practice.

RAW JUICING: THE HEALTHY, EASY, AND DELICIOUS WAY TO GAIN THE BENEFITS
OF THE RAW FOOD LIFESTYLE
Leslie Kenton, $12.95
As the health benefits of eating uncooked food become widely acknowledged, more
people are looking for ways to "go raw" (at least for some meals). This book's raw-juice
plan and great-tasting recipes offer the easiest way to "go raw" for a meal: make a super-
healthy, delicious raw juice drink.

*To order these books call 800-377-2542 or 510-601-8301, fax 510-601-8307, e-mail
ulysses@ulyssespress.com, or write to Ulysses Press, P.O. Box 3440, Berkeley, CA 94703. All
retail orders are shipped free of charge. California residents must include sales tax. Allow two to
three weeks for delivery.*

❧ ABOUT THE AUTHOR

KELLY E. KEOUGH is an expert healthy chef, author, and host of *The Sweet Truth* cooking show on Veria TV. Kelly's passion is inspiring people with health, weight, and aging concerns related to sugar and gluten to not live without—but to have their sweets and eat them, too. Kelly's mission is to dedicate herself to educating people about sugar-free, gluten-free alternative ingredients and superfoods and to show families how easy it is to be healthy so they can benefit from her unique food philosophy and baking style. She lives in Los Angeles, California. Visit www.kellykeough.com for more information on Kelly and a sugar-free, gluten-free diet.